FIESTA

FIESTA

DAYS OF THE DEAD
& OTHER MEXICAN FESTIVALS

Chloë Sayer

THE BRITISH MUSEUM PRESS

frontispiece
Small girl by a decorative archway for Our Lady of Guadalupe
in the Nahua village of Zoatecpan, Puebla state, 1994
(photo: C. Sayer)

below
Detail of a gigantic papier mâché Judas figure made for Holy
Week by Leonardo Linares Vargas, 1992 (see p. 102)

© 2009 The Trustees of the British Museum

Chloë Sayer has asserted the moral right
to be identified as the author of this work

First published in 2009 by The British Museum Press
A division of The British Museum Company Ltd
38 Russell Square, London WC1B 3QQ
www.britishmuseum.org

A catalogue record for this book is available
from the British Library

ISBN 978-0-7141-2588-6

Designed and typeset in Futura and Minion by Turchini
Design Ltd
Photography by the British Museum Department of
Photography and Imaging (unless otherwise noted)
Printed and bound in Singapore by Tien Wah Press Ltd

Contents

Introduction

Mexico has a vast range of festivals. While some commemorate national events, the majority are religious in inspiration. These draw heavily on the Christian legacy of colonial rule, but even today perceptions and practices owe much to Mexico's pre-Christian past. When Spanish *conquistadores* reached central Mexico in 1520, they saw the civilization of the Aztecs (who called themselves the Mexica) at its height. This explains why the beliefs and festivals of the Aztecs were better documented than those of their predecessors and contemporaries, who shared similar spiritual traditions.

The term 'Mesoamerica' is widely used to define a cultural area which includes a large part of Mexico. According to the anthropologist Paul Kirchhoff, who proposed this classification in 1943, Mesoamerica incorporates the southern two-thirds of Mexico, all of Belize, Guatemala and El Salvador, and parts of Honduras, Nicaragua and Costa Rica. Cultural traits shared by the inhabitants of this vast area included long-distance trade, well-organized markets, intensive agriculture, solar and ritual calendars, and a complex pantheon of deities. In this interrelated world, local and regional populations exchanged their ideas and their material culture over long periods of time.

Aztec festivals, many dedicated to the gods of rain and maize, depended on Mesoamerican calendrical cycles. Celebrated with visual splendour and a wealth of symbolic elements, festivals were often preceded by preparatory rites and followed by concluding ceremonies. The ritual agricultural cycle was punctuated by key dates marking the start of the Aztec year on 12

opposite left
Ceremonial candelabrum of painted pottery in the form of a 'tree of life' from Izúcar de Matamoros, Puebla state, late 1980s. The maker, Heriberto Castillo Orta, comes of a long line of ceramic artists. The musicians and some decorative elements are supported by short lengths of wire; the female figure at the base displays a painted cross. Ht 64 cm.

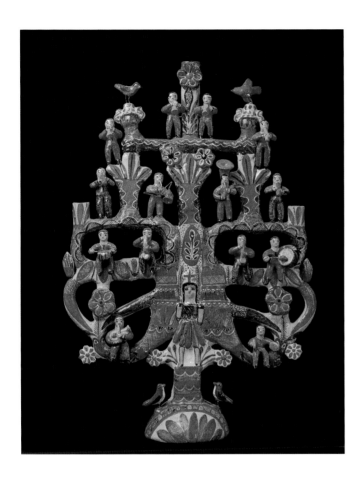

right

Painting from the Nahua village of Ameyaltepec, Guerrero state, late 1980s. Inspired by Christian beliefs and done on *amate* (bark paper) by Telésforo Rodríguez Lusino, it shows village life on earth: celebrants visit the cemetery on All Souls' Day. Above, in the heavens, angels accompany the sun (represented by the all-seeing eye of God) and the crescent moon. Hell and the flames of eternal damnation are shown below. Ht 117.5 cm.

February, the planting of maize on 30 April, the climax of the rainy season and the growth of maize plants on 13 August, and the harvest on 30 October. The Mesoamerican world view was based on the need to control opposing forces: the gods, neither purely good nor purely evil, often had dual aspects. Human sacrifice ensured the daily appearance of the sun and the renewal of fertility. According to Johanna Broda, who has analysed Aztec ritual, 'humans tried to control ritually the balance of the forces of nature and to propitiate them for their own benefit'. She also notes that, 'in the manner of a fugue, a web of ceremonies was created which spanned the whole year and led from one celebration to the next'.

Spain's epic conquest of the Aztec empire was completed in 1521. This was followed by the overthrow of the Tarascan empire of western Mexico, the oppression of the peoples of Oaxaca, and the eventual subjugation of the Maya populations of the Yucatán Peninsula and Guatemala. The arrival in 1535 of the first viceroy marked the start of the colonial period in New Spain, as Mexico became officially known. Under the system of *encomienda*, Spanish colonists were granted a right to the labour and tribute of indigenous populations. The harsh conditions of Spanish-run mines and plantations, combined with epidemics of introduced European diseases such as measles, led to numerous deaths. Demographic estimates are much debated, but many experts now accept that 80 per cent

of the indigenous population may have perished during the sixteenth century. Spanish settlers, faced with acute labour shortages, imported approximately 36,000 African slaves between 1521 and 1594. *Encomienda* was later replaced by great *haciendas* (estates), where exploitation often verged on serfdom. Mexican independence from Spain was achieved in 1821.

The contradictions underlying the early years of Spanish rule were many. Based on private enterprise, the conquest was carried out by brave and ambitious men eager to reap a financial reward. The Crown also required its percentage of all revenue, officially termed the Royal Fifth. Charles V was not only king of Spain, however. As emperor of the Holy Roman Empire, it was his moral duty to justify military conquest in terms of religious conversion. Churches and monasteries were erected, often on the sites of earlier shrines. Indigenous books were burned and idols smashed. During the first fifty years of colonial rule, the mission of conversion was carried out in large part by orders of Mendicant friars who, inspired by the simplicity of early Christianity, took vows of poverty.

The Franciscans were the first to propagate the Christian faith, often using theatrical representation as a method of instruction. Soon they were joined by the Dominicans, the Augustinians and, in the 1570s, the Jesuits. The annual cycle of Roman Catholic festivities, celebrated throughout New Spain, included feast days for the Virgin Mary and other important saints. Christian ideas about heaven, hell and purgatory were alien concepts. Although pre-Conquest populations believed in an afterlife, this was not seen as a reward or punishment for deeds done in life. The devil similarly lacked meaning in a land where supernatural forces were never regarded as wholly malevolent. The missionary orders, with evangelical zeal, imported the European custom of staging 'morality' plays and allegorical pageants to dramatize the Christian abstractions of virtue and sin.

above
The baroque church of San Francisco Acatepec, Puebla state, decorated in readiness for the Day of St Francis in 1994.

opposite above
Performers representing Moors and Christians outside the former Dominican convent of Tepoztlán, Morelos state, in 1983. Introduced into Mexico after the Conquest, *la danza de los moros y cristianos* is still widely performed.

opposite below
Church archways created from flowers and foliage to honour St Matthew the Apostle in 1998 in Metepec, Mexico state.

Over time most indigenous populations adopted Christianity, but this acceptance was often coloured by residual indigenous beliefs. Agricultural rituals were incorporated into the annual Catholic cycle; Christian saints took on the traits of pre-Christian deities. As late as 1803, an entire town in the Valley of Mexico was found to be worshipping idols in secret caves. This process has been much discussed by anthropologists and historians. William Madsen coined the term 'Christo-paganism' and embraced the idea of pre-Hispanic continuity; other scholars prefer to focus on the Christian legacy, whereas Hugo Nutini wisely observes that, 'when two religious systems meet … the resultant religious system is different from the two original interacting systems …' Modern Mexico, with its wealth of spiritual beliefs and customs, has a festive calendar that few places can equal. To re-use Johanna Broda's words in a contemporary context, the year is still 'spanned' by 'a web of ceremonies'.

Festivities for Our Lady of Guadalupe, Mexico's patron saint, culminate on 12 December. The Christmas cycle, which follows immediately, ends on

above
The figure of the Virgin Mary is carried through the streets of Pahuatlán, Puebla state, during Holy Week in 1986.

left
Weaver Crispina Navarro Gómez (see pp. 113–14) with her sister Margarita beside an *ofrenda* or altar for the Days of the Dead in 2008. Like their neighbours in Santo Tomás Jalieza, Oaxaca state, they welcome the returning souls with offerings of fruit and flowers.

opposite
Pair of papier mâché figures made in Mexico City in 1989 by Leonardo Linares Vargas. The devil and the avenging angel of death are shown in mortal combat. Ht (left) 34 cm, (right) 55 cm.

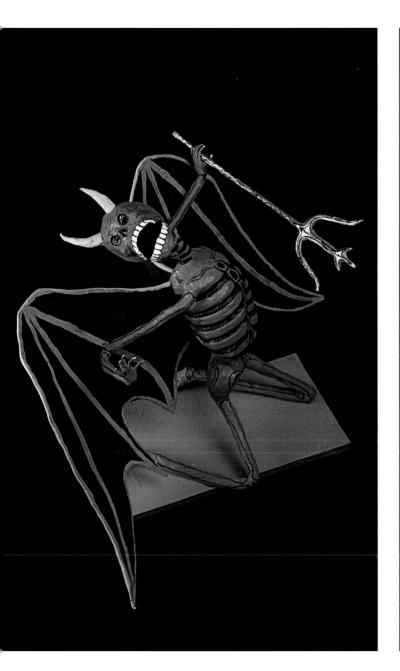

left
Bullfighting scene of painted wood, made in
Arrazola, Oaxaca state, during the mid 1980s.
Ht (*torero*) 20 cm.

below
Painted pottery candle holder with St Michael the
Archangel, made in 1989 in Huaquechula, Puebla
state. Ceremonial pottery of this type is used on
altars during the Days of the Dead. Ht 30 cm.

2 February with Candlemas. Carnival, Lent and Holy Week represent a single group of events, and coincide with the start of the planting season. On 3 May, Day of the Holy Cross, mountain and roadside crosses are adorned with flowers. In Huaquechula, Puebla state, groups of worshippers dance with baskets of food and flowers in front of public shrines inset with crosses. Because 3 May is also the day of masons, unfinished buildings everywhere display crosses, flowers and coloured streamers. The moveable feast of Corpus Christi, in late May or June, commemorates the Last Supper and honours the Holy Eucharist. Children are often dressed in indigenous clothing; they may also be given a small *huacal* (crate) or *ayate* (carrying cloth) hung with miniaturized implements for traditional tasks. *Mulitas* (tiny mules), made from sticks and maize husks, are loaded with sweets.

Remembrance is central to the Festival of the Dead, which has strong links with the harvest. On 1 and 2 November (All Saints' and All Souls'), the living honour the souls of the departed with gifts of food and flowers. These offerings are carefully set out, near revered holy images and pictures of saints, on the household altar. In some regions celebrations last longer. The souls of dead children may be welcomed back on 31 October; infants who die before baptism (*los limbos*) are sometimes thought to return on 30 October, preceded by the adult victims of drowning, accidents or violence. Other *fiesta* dates in the annual cycle are determined by local saints' days. After the Conquest, each settlement was assigned a patron saint. On 15 August lavish festivities for the Virgin of the Assumption take place in towns, villages and *barrios* (neighbourhoods) called Santa María. Those named after San Marcos, Santa Mónica or San Francisco celebrate on 25 April, 27 August and 4 October respectively.

Festivals and fairs, if celebrated in large towns, attract thousands of visitors. Travelling funfairs, with their Ferris wheels and roundabouts, are always popular. Attractions include games like *la lotería* (the lottery). Players

below

Printed game-board showing cards for *la lotería* (the lottery). Although this version was printed during the 1980s, the images are considerably older. 12.5 x 9 cm (each card).

are given cards with pictures rather than numbers. These include images of death, the devil, the mermaid and the *nopal* (prickly pear); usually the names are called in rhyme. Wrestling matches take place in makeshift tents, and sideshows display curiosities and cautionary *tableaux*: from inside her box of mirrors, the *mujer-serpiente* (serpent-woman) explains to wide-eyed children that she became this way after disobeying her parents. *Jaripeos* (rodeos), cockfights and bullfights also provide festive entertainment.

In regions where indigenous cultures are especially strong, festivals take on a unique character. According to the national census of 2005, indigenous languages are spoken by approximately six million people aged five years or over. A larger number probably regard themselves as indigenous, because of shared community ties and traditions. The Zoque live in northwestern Chiapas and adjoining areas of Tabasco and Oaxaca. According to the anthropologist Frank J. Lipp Jr, they have combined Jesus with an earlier sun deity; the Virgin Mary is identified with a moon

Male Nahua performers in 1985 outside the church in Xalpatzingo, Puebla state. During *la danza de los negritos*, inspired long ago by African slaves, performers represent field-workers; one is bitten by a snake. Over-trousers are richly embroidered. Hats are adorned with mirrors, rosettes of metallic foil and 'fibreglass' plumes; a heavy fringe hangs down over the performers' faces.

left
Masks of painted papier mâché from the town of Celaya, Guanajuato state, mid 1970s. As Carnival approaches, makers use traditional moulds to create a range of faces with human, animal or supernatural features. However, factory-produced rubber masks or wrestling masks are increasingly replacing more traditional masks. Ht (left) 23 cm, (right) 21 cm.

below
St Peter, patron saint of San Pedro Ocumicho, Michoacán, mid 1970s. Represented here in painted pottery, he is brought out of the church on his feast day to preside over dances performed in his honour. Ht 37 cm.

goddess closely related to lunar phases and their influence on the growth of crops. Zoque Christmas celebrations have important links with agriculture; in one community, for example, maize is ritually grown inside a special house with a decorated altar. On 24 December this shrine becomes a focus for ceremonial activities. Women process carrying seeds for planting. Offerings of seeds, herbs and candles are made at the altar. A manger is fashioned from strings of flowers, and the Christ-child is carried from house to house. The Totonac, who live in the state of Veracruz, give great importance to the Days of the Dead. *Ninín*, to use their term, runs from the Day of San Lucas on 18 October to the Day of San Andrés on 30 November. Holy Week celebrations among the Tarahumara, the Cora and the Mayo are described in a later chapter.

Extensive preparations precede even the simplest of ceremonies. Cloths for wrapping food are woven or embroidered. Delicate banners are perforated by the paper-cutters of San Salvador Huixcolotla, in Puebla state, where sharp chisels are hammered through layers of coloured paper to create festive designs. Candle holders and incense burners are made by specialist potters. In Huaquechula, these are brightly painted and decorated with angels and saints. In Metepec, in the state of Mexico, they are glazed a rich black for the Days of the Dead. Candles, made from beeswax or paraffin, are European in origin. Native incense, termed *copal*, is an aromatic resin extracted from trees of the genus *Bursera*. Ceremonial and festive items are sold at seasonal markets. In late October, an immense fair is held in Huancito, Michoacán. On display are whistles, money-banks and other ceramic toys from the Purépecha village of Ocumicho. Sugar figures for the returning souls are laid out in colourful profusion in Pátzcuaro, Oaxaca City, San Miguel Allende and Toluca. Nativity figures for Christmas, papier mâché masks for Carnival and 'Judas' figures for Holy Week also travel long distances from their places of origin.

During Mexican festivals, perishable materials are deployed with ingenuity and skill. In Metepec, magnificent archways of leaves and flowers are built round the entrances of churches and atria. Paths of flower petals and dyed sawdust lead through the village of Patamban, Michoacán, for the Feast of Cristo Rey (Christ the King). In Mazahua churches in the state of Mexico, holy images are embellished with festoons of threaded popcorn; saints may be hung with garlands of flowers and Marie biscuits. Large and delicate candles of moulded wax, sometimes shimmering with layers of metallic paper, are displayed in churches in and around Cuetzalan, Puebla. Because remote villages are often without a resident priest, care of the church and its saints may rest with the local community. Motivated by an intense sense of connection, inhabitants lavish time and money on this sacred task. Differences with priests, resident or otherwise, are not unknown. As local people explain, the priest will leave when his term of office ends whereas they are the true custodians.

above
On the Day of St Peter in 1984, the Mazahua inhabitants of San Pedro de la Loma, Mexico state, process with the image of their patron saint. He is garlanded with flowers and hung with a necklace of Marie biscuits.

opposite left
Zapotec women processing through the streets of Tehuantepec, Oaxaca state, in 2006. The outlying ward of Santa María Reoloteca holds its chief festivity on 15 August, Feast of the Assumption – the day Mary was received into heaven. Celebrants carry ceremonial banners and painted bowls full of fruit.

Processions, whether in large towns or tiny villages, are an important component of religious life. Richly decorated and wearing their finest attire, the saints are carried along the ceremonial route. Some communities organize *carros alegóricos*. These *tableaux vivants* on the backs of lorries represent scenes from the lives of the saints. On 22 May, for example, Santa Rita may be impersonated by a local girl. Taped to her forehead is a gigantic nail: this represents the thorn that fell from a figure of the crucified Christ

above

Totonac performance of *el palo volador* (the flying pole) at El Tajín, Veracruz state, in 1978. During their descent, the four *voladores* (flyers) complete a total of 52 turns. The musician, who remains on the platform at the top, plays a reed flute and small drum.

and wounded the fifteenth-century saint. The day of San Isidro Labrador, on 15 May, is a big occasion in Metepec. Large pictures, partially painted and partially composed as a mosaic of seeds, show agricultural scenes from the life of St Isidore, patron saint of farmers. Once these images were carried through the streets by teams of oxen; today motorized vehicles are preferred. Although the festival has a serious intention, it is leavened with fun and burlesque as small boys and young men cross-dress to assume the role of 'women'.

Many celebrations are still dominated by dances, which vary according to region. Indigenous communities in the states of Veracruz and Puebla give great importance to their festive traditions. Pre-Conquest in origin, the ceremony of *el palo volador* (the flying pole) was performed as a calendrical ritual by dancers wearing feathered wings. Contemporary Totonac and Nahua performers no longer impersonate birds, but other ancient observances have been retained. Although some villages now use a concrete pole, a few still select and fell their tree with care; offerings are placed in the vacant hole. Positioned near the church in the main square, the stripped trunk or concrete pole is given a revolving platform at its summit. On the day of the ceremony four *voladores* (fliers), accompanied by a musician, dance several times round the base of the pole. They then climb a knotted rope to reach the platform. Each *volador* ties himself by the waist to a large wooden spool. The musician, who remains on the

above

Nahua performers taking part in *la danza de los quetzales* to honour the Virgin of Guadalupe on 12 December 1994 in Cuetzalan, Puebla state.

opposite

Nahua headdress for the dance of the *guaguas* (sometimes called *quetzalines*) from Cuetzalan, Puebla state, 1985. Ht 74 cm.

platform, plays a reed flute and a small drum. When the *voladores* fling themselves into space, their ropes unwind. Each of the four fliers circles the pole thirteen times before reaching the ground. The total number of turns is fifty-two, representing the fifty-two-year cycle of the Mesoamerican 'Calendar Round', produced by combining a solar calendar of 365 days with a sacred calendar of 260 days.

Nahua dancers in and around Cuetzalan perform another probably ancient dance: *los quetzales*. Immense headdresses are worn, inspired perhaps by the plumage of the quetzal bird. These are made by specialists who create a circular framework of stiff reeds, interlaced with multicoloured paper and strips of ribbon; small feathers decorate the tips of spokes. With precise timing, dancers holding gourd rattles mark out the four cardinal points of the compass with the right foot; they then stamp and rotate. A similar but smaller headdress is worn by *guagua* dancers, sometimes called *quetzalines*, who rotate on a high wheel supported by two vertical wooden posts.

The fusion of indigenous and Spanish masking traditions has given rise over time to numerous dances in which the chief performers are masked. Wood is the raw material most often used, and mask-carvers often double as *santeros* (saint-makers). Alternative materials include leather, clay, paper, cloth, wire mesh, gourds and wax. Because most masks are scaled to fit the human face, wearers look through narrow slits above or below the eyes of the mask. If the mask is unusually large, the dancer's sightline may be through the open mouth. Many masks represent creatures from the animal world; these often have links with hunting, fishing and agricultural ceremonies. In northern Mexico, during *la danza del venado* (Deer Dance), Yaqui and Mayo performers simulate a hunt which ends with the death of the deer.

The majority of Mexican masks show human faces with male features. While some have indigenous traits, others represent different races.

above
In the Nahua village of Acapetlahuaya, Guerrero state, Fidel Navarro is respected for his skill both as a *santero* (saint-carver) and as a maker of masks for local dances. 1988.

opposite
Zapotec women in 2004 wearing richly embroidered clothing for the Feast of the Assumption in Santa María Reoloteca, Tehuantepec, Oaxaca state. Most celebrants commission a new ensemble for the festival each year.

Elegantly dressed Black Africans appear in various dances. In pre-Hispanic Mexico, the colour black was associated with several powerful deities. According to Janet Brody Esser, who has studied Mexican masking traditions, *negros* (Blackmen) are thought by the Purépecha of Michoacán to represent superhuman lords or 'principal beings who control the air'. Europeans, with their fair skins, facial hair and blue or green eyes, are frequently portrayed. Two important dance cycles – *moros y cristianos* (Moors and Christians) and *la conquista* (the Conquest) – show Spanish soldiers defending their homeland against Moorish invasion or gaining victory over the peoples of ancient Mexico. In Michoacán, where *moros* sometimes perform alone, their unmasked faces are partially covered by a kerchief; garments are profusely trimmed with sequins and gilt braid. Women took part in a number of dances before the Conquest. In sixteenth-century Europe, by contrast, female roles were generally played by young men. Today, during Mexican festivals, female masks and clothing are widely worn by men who perform as female characters.

Masked supernatural beings appear in allegorical dances of European origin such as *los siete vicios* (the Seven Vices) and *las tres potencias* (the Three Powers). Angels, death, the devil and the deadly sins still do battle at *fiesta* time in the village squares of Guerrero and other states. Ritual clowning was a component of pre-Conquest festivals. The devil was an alien presence in

New Spain, and many contemporary dances cast him as a ceremonial buffoon. Humour may also be generated by performers impersonating death, and by several non-supernatural figures: these often include 'female' characters and the elderly (*viejos*) who cavort and hobble on sticks. Extreme seriousness, by contrast, attaches to the figure of Santiago Apóstol (St James the Apostle). As the patron saint and special protector of the Spanish *conquistadores*, St James was portrayed on horseback in colonial church paintings and sculpture. Horses, unknown in the New World, were initially seen as supernatural by some indigenous populations. During contemporary *conquista* dances that celebrate the arrival of Christianity, St James often wears a white-painted wooden horse at his waist.

below
Musicians of painted pottery from Metepec, Mexico state, part of a larger funeral group (see p. 125), late 1980s. Ht (average) 17 cm.

When dance masks are removed from their ceremonial context, perhaps for display in museums and galleries, it is easy to forget the veneration they command. As in so many places, Nahua villagers near Cuetzalan regard their role as sacred. Each outgoing Santiago entrusts the carved dance horse to his successor. Thought to be endowed with life, the horse lives on the household altar where it is offered maize and water. Although cheerfulness and humour are essential ingredients during most Mexican festivals, the underlying purpose is wholly serious. Often dancers perform because of a *manda*: this is a sacred vow made to God and the saints. The performer, perhaps in gratitude for divine help and intercession, promises to take part in the dance for a fixed number of years. He must assume the costs, which are often high, of costume and mask; he must give up time for rehearsals and learn any necessary lines. Whether dances are ancient like *los voladores*, or recognizably European like *moros y cristianos*, performers believe they are taking part in an act of worship. Where survival depends on agriculture, dancers seek on behalf of their community to ensure the success of the harvest and the harmonious succession of the seasons. As in pre-Conquest times, purification and sacrifice are paramount.

Before the Conquest a rhythmic accompaniment to dances was provided by reed and clay flutes, conch shells, grooved bones, upright and horizontal drums, and gourd rattles. Stringed and brass instruments were introduced during the colonial era. Musicians in modern Mexico, unlike dancers, charge for their services. Their fees and other outgoings are often covered by *mayordomos* or 'patrons' who voluntarily sponsor festivities. In indigenous communities, families who are better off than their neighbours regard it as a sacred duty to fund religious events. Meals may be offered over several days to dancers and musicians in the home of the *mayordomo*. Celebrations often culminate in a display of fireworks. An immense cane *castillo* (castle) is constructed near the church. When darkness descends,

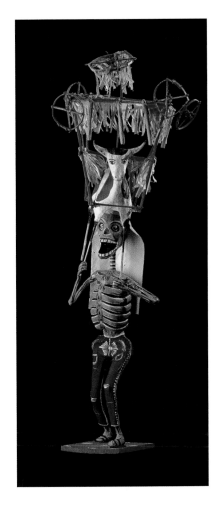

Skeleton *torero* of wire and papier mâché with paper decorations, made in the mid 1970s by Pedro Linares Jiménez of Mexico City. During many Mexican festivities, the figure of a *torito* (little bull) is fitted with fireworks and carried on the shoulders. Ht (skeleton) 55 cm.

rockets and Catherine wheels fill the sky with cascades of light and colour. Firework-bedecked *toritos* (little bulls) are also popular: boys and young men cover their heads and shoulders with bull-shaped armatures of cane and papier mâché. When the touch-paper is lit and the fireworks ignite, the 'bulls' run at the crowd.

In addition to public *fiestas*, private celebrations also punctuate the Mexican year. As in other countries, baptisms, confirmations and weddings are important rites of passage. The *santo* (saint's day) has more significance than a birthday. Anyone named after Santa Cecilia or San Ernesto, for example, will celebrate on 21 October or 7 November. There is one exceptionally important birthday in each girl's life, however. When she enters maturity on her fifteenth birthday, *la quinceañera* attends a thanksgiving mass accompanied by her *damas* (maids of honour), godparents and family. Her bouquet is offered to the Virgin Mary. Festivities, as Octavio Paz has noted, are central to life in Mexico. In *El laberinto de la soledad*, the celebrated essayist and poet explains: 'Fiestas are our sole luxury ... What is important is to go out, open up a way, get drunk on noise, people, colours. Mexico is in fiesta.'

opposite
Carnival festivities in 1986 in the Otomí (nyûhû) village of San Pablito near Pahuatlán, Puebla state. Male dancers dress as 'women', their identity concealed by scarves and dark glasses. They perform to the music of the guitar (played by Pedro Laja) and the fiddle.

below
Handmade wedding banner of perforated tissue paper, commissioned by the bridegroom in 1989 from Maurilio Rojas of San Salvador Huixcolotla, Puebla state. 73 x 48 cm.

The Sacred Art of the Huichol

What beautiful hills, what beautiful hills,
so green here where we are.
Do not weep, brothers, do not weep,
we have come here to be happy,
we have taken this path
to find our lives.

For we are all,
we are all the children
of a flower of brilliant colours,
of a burning flower.
And here there is no one
who regrets what we are ...

Sacred Huichol song in honour of Wirikuta
(recorded by Peter T. Furst and Barbara E. Myerhoff)

eligion permeated every aspect of life in pre-Hispanic times, and this is still the case in indigenous Mexico today. But whereas most populations have been heavily influenced by Christianity, the Huichol have preserved their ideology and their ceremonies virtually intact. Collective belief finds expression in a year-long cycle of festivals and pilgrimages. These focus on a complex pantheon of nature and ancestor deities. It is the responsibility of shamans, who are able to enter the spirit world after due preparation, to protect and restore the delicate equilibrium between human beings and the spiritual and natural worlds.

Cut off from the outside world by the mountain ranges and deep canyons of the western Sierra Madre, Huichol territory lies at the intersection of four states: Jalisco, Nayarit, Durango and Zacatecas. Because there is a scarcity of arable land, slash-and-burn farming is often practised on semi-vertical hillsides. Land, situated at an average elevation of 2000 m (6560 ft), is communally owned. Extended families live in small, widely scattered settlements. Huichol society is highly ordered: the territory is divided into five independent areas, each with its own administrative and ceremonial centre. Despite the precarious nature of existence, the Huichol population has increased from an estimated total of around 5000 in 1902 to an estimated total of 44,000 in 2000.

The Huichol speak a Uto-Aztecan language and refer to themselves as the Wixaritari (Wixárika in the singular). This term has been variously translated as 'prophets' and 'healers', although research by the campaigner Juan Negrín Fetter suggests that it might mean 'He who clothes himself in

above
Detail of a female celebrant from a 'yarn painting', early 1970s (overleaf).

opposite
Huichol mask of carved wood with painted motifs from Jalisco state, early 1970s. Although masks are rarely worn by Huichol celebrants, a simple wooden mask is sometimes used during festivities for the First Fruits: the wearer takes the role of a sacred buffoon. This mask was probably made for sale to outsiders. Designs replicate the facial markings favoured by *peyote*-pilgrims. Ht 24 cm.

honour of our ancestors'. The Franciscans tried unsuccessfully to convert the Huichol to Christianity in the 1730s, then abandoned their missions and withdrew. Recent attempts by outsiders to influence the Huichol have been similarly rebuffed. When the Norwegian anthropologist Carl Lumholtz spent time with the Huichol in the 1890s, he noted: 'Never for a moment will a Huichol allow that any other race may be superior to his own. Even when far from home among the whites, the Huichol will bear themselves as if they had never known masters.' Today, more than a century later, the Huichol take the same pride in their heritage.

Collectively, Huichol deities are referred to as *kakauyarite.* According to Peter T. Furst, who has devoted several decades to researching Huichol culture, there is no satisfactory translation for this term. Addressed by ritual kinship terms, deities within the extensive Huichol pantheon include the sun god, 'Our Father' Tayaupá, and the fertility goddess, 'Our Great-grandmother' Nakawé. A number of other female deities, regarded as 'Our Mothers', are identified with rain, earth, growth and maize. The fire god, 'Our Grandfather' Tatewarí, is the patron of shamans. The principal spirit helper of shamans

opposite
Huichol 'yarn painting' from Jalisco state, early 1970s. Father Sun presides over a ceremony conducted in his honour by two shamans seated on ceremonial chairs near the temple. They are surrounded by ritual paraphernalia. 82.5 x 121 cm.

below
Carved wooden deer fitted with real horns and covered with imported glass beads. The serpent symbolizes lightning. Made by Francisco Carrillo Zamora in Tepic, Nayarit state, *c.* 1995. Ht 25 cm.

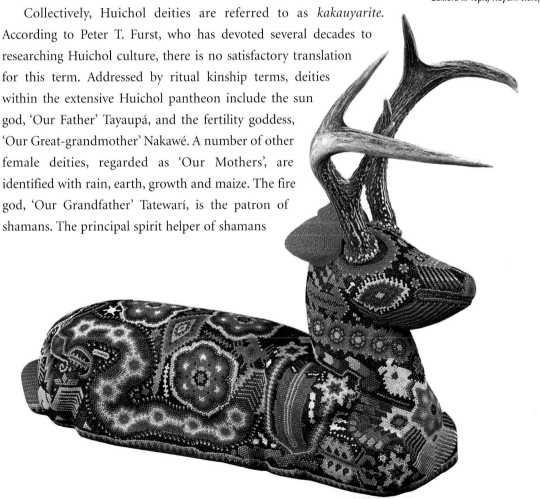

Children participate during *la fiesta del tambor* (Feast of the Drum) to celebrate the First Fruits in San Andrés Cohamiata, Jalisco state, 1978. The little girl has painted yellow facial markings. The shaman, wearing richly embroidered clothing, sits between his two assistants. Sacred arrows, 'planted' in the earth, carry prayers to the gods.

Votive half-gourd lined with glass beads to show scorpions; the design in the centre symbolizes *peyote*. Early 1970s. Diam. 17 cm.

is Kauyumári, 'Our Elder Brother Deer Person', who acts as an intermediary between the Huichol and their deities. Gods and goddesses manifest themselves as natural features throughout Huichol territory and beyond. They are also honoured in *tuki* (circular temples with thatched roofs) in the main ceremonial centres. These temples are tended by a succession of officials, or *cargo*-holders, who are required to settle near the *tuki* for their period of service.

The *mara'akáme* (shaman) is the fire god's human counterpart. His role is extremely demanding, intellectually and physically. It is his duty to sing sacred songs, preside over ceremonies and

During the Feast of the First Fruits the Huichol give thanks to their gods. Offerings include ripe squash, maize cobs, *tamales* and candles. Huichol shoulder-bags are embroidered in cross stitch (left) or double-woven on the backstrap loom (right). San Andrés Cohamiata, Jalisco state, 1978.

pilgrimages, and deposit prayer offerings at sacred places throughout the landscape. He is the custodian of Huichol beliefs, moral values and oral history. Responsible for the spiritual and physical well-being of followers, he must relieve individual sickness and community afflictions. According to Peter T. Furst, a growing number of women are now sufficiently versed in esoteric lore and healing techniques to become fully accepted shamans, and some have already done so.

The Huichol year is defined by a number of festivals corresponding to the wet and dry seasons. These are often held in the main ceremonial centres. Quiet and virtually deserted throughout most of the year, these centres are filled during festive periods by large groups of celebrants who have walked through the Sierra, laden with food and offerings. Important events are often preceded by a deer hunt. During festivals, the Huichol sometimes offer their deities the blood of a sacrificed rooster or bull. Because the Huichol are dependent for their survival on maize, they hold numerous ceremonies to honour its various stages of growth. Other agricultural events include the Feast of the First Fruits, when the faithful give thanks for the new harvest. Gifts are offered to the gods: these include squash, *tamales* (steamed cakes of maize dough), and finely made shoulder-bags filled with ripe maize cobs.

In the dry season, parties of Huichol pilgrims travel long distances to find Tatéi Hikuri, 'Our Mother Peyote'. Identified with the deer and with maize, this hallucinatory cactus inspires the Huichol throughout their lives. The cult of this small grey-green plant, known to botanists as *Lophophora williamsii*, has a long history in Mexico. We know from Fray Bernardino de Sahagún, the sixteenth-century Franciscan chronicler, that the nomadic Teochichimeca of the northern deserts held *peyote* ceremonies during which they would weep. Wirikuta, the sacred place where *peyote* grows, lies far outside

Generally made for sale to collectors, Huichol 'yarn paintings' show scenes from ceremonial and religious life. Stylized motifs include *peyote*, the deer, and offerings such as candles, votive arrows and the shaman's sacred wand of bird feathers.

opposite above
'Yarn painting' made by Francisco Carrillo Zamora in Tepic, Nayarit state, *c.* 1995. 60 x 60 cm.

opposite below
'Yarn painting' made by José Carrillo Cosío in Jalisco state, *c.* 1996. 40 x 40 cm.

below
Detail from a 'yarn painting', early 1970s (see p. 28).

Huichol territory in the desert of San Luis Potosí. The arduous journey is preceded and accompanied throughout by purification rites, fasting and other voluntary hardships. According to Huichol lore, *peyote* first appeared on earth as a giant deer. Because the quest parallels a hunting ritual, the first *peyote* cactus is ritually 'slain' with a bow and arrow. Those who go in search of *peyote* must also gather *uxa* – the root of the desert laurel. Later, ground and mixed with water, it will provide the Huichol with the yellow liquid needed to paint faces and objects with sacred symbols. The return of the *peyoteros* (*peyote*-pilgrims) is celebrated by the community at large. *Peyote*, eaten fresh or dried for later use, has a high mescaline content. Those who take it agree that it is extremely bitter, but say they are rewarded by brilliantly coloured visions, heightened perception and a sense of euphoria. Shamans often use *peyote* when communicating with the spirit world.

Another important site of pilgrimage lies on the coast near San Blas, in the state of Nayarit. This is where the Huichol locate the entrance to the underworld, and offerings are left in a rock shelter. Pilgrims go to the water's edge to pay their respects to Tatéi Haramara, goddess of the Pacific Ocean. Children on a first visit are often blindfolded during the last part of the journey; only when they reach the ocean are the blindfolds removed. Many pilgrims spend an entire night on the beach, waiting for the sun to rise. In the early light of dawn, they enter the sea. Gourds and other offerings may be floated on the waves.

Highly creative, the Huichol dedicate immense skill and unlimited time to the elaboration of clothing and ritual objects. Garments of bought cotton cloth are covered with cross-stitched motifs. Bags and belts, woven on the back-strap loom, display a wealth of patterning. Double-headed eagles and deer are often shown; *peyote* is represented as a stylized flower. Because clothing has a spiritual as well as a functional role, designs serve as visual prayers that protect the wearer from harm. Small glass beads, adopted many

opposite
Huichol pilgrims from the mountain community of Tierras Blancas pay their respects to Tatéi Haramara, goddess of the Pacific Ocean, in October 1996. After spending the night on the beach near San Blas, they enter the water. It is thought that everyone should make this pilgrimage at least once.

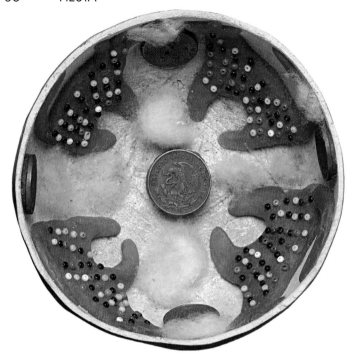

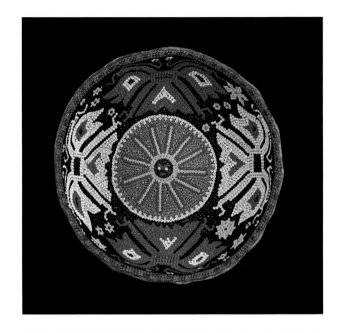

The Huichol seek to win the goodwill of their gods with offerings such as votive bowls. It is hoped that the gods will drink in the prayers of the faithful and grant their requests.

above
Old-style gourd bowl displaying wads of cotton wool, a Mexican coin, and wax figures of deer inset with glass beads. Early 1970s. Diam. (approx.) 11 cm.

right
These two half-gourds are entirely lined with wax. Imported glass beads have been pressed down one by one on the point of a needle to form eagles, deer, *peyote* symbols and other sacred designs. Diam. (above) 16.5 cm, (below) 25 cm.

decades ago by the Huichol, are used to make netted beadwork armbands, pectorals and ear ornaments.

Votive offerings for the gods include gourd bowls, lined with wax and decorated with coins and tufts of cotton. Some makers press glass beads into the wax to form pictures of deer, suns, birds and plants. Religious devotion finds another outlet in the *nierika* ('countenance'). Fashioned from stone, from reeds interwoven with thread, or from small wooden boards covered with wax and yarn, these round or square offerings provide an abstract or representational vision of the spiritual and the supernatural. Yarn 'paintings', initially inspired by the *nierika*, have been made commercially for several decades. Strands of wool, pressed down on to wax-covered boards, show *peyote* visions and complex scenes from Huichol mythology and ceremonial life. Bought by museums and collectors, they provide a creative outlet for makers and bring in much-needed revenue.

In recent years, many Huichol families have moved away from the Sierra to settle in Tepic. Others pay long visits to Mexico City, Guadalajara and Puerto Vallarta. Physical removal from Huichol territory does not entail a loss of religious faith, however. Close emotional ties are still maintained with Wirikuta and with the sacred landscape of home. Huichol daily life remains 'indivisible from religion', just as it was in the 1890s when Carl Lumholtz documented Huichol culture. In order to win the protection and goodwill of their gods, the Huichol are still prepared to make offerings, vows and sacrifices. Privation and hardship are balanced by an intense spiritual awareness and constant contact with the divine.

below
Carved wooden figure of a *peyote* cactus, covered with glass beads. This sacred hallucinatory plant is identified by the Huichol with deer and maize. Made by Francisco Carrillo Zamora in Tepic, Nayarit state, *c.* 1995. Ht 8 cm.

The Blessed Virgin Mary:
Nuestra Señora de Guadalupe

Buenos días, paloma blanca,
Hoy te vengo a saludar,
Saludando a tu belleza
En tu reino celestial.

Eres guía del marinero,
Eres estrella del mar,
En la tierra y en el cielo
Yo te vengo a saludar.

Good morning, white dove,
Today I come to greet you,
Greeting your beauty
In your celestial reign.

You are the sailor's guide,
You are the star of the sea,
On earth and in heaven
I come to greet you.

Popular hymn to the Virgin Mary

The story of the Virgin Mary in the New World began in 1492 with the first voyage of Christopher Columbus. The name of his flagship was the *Santa María*, and its main sail bore an image of the Virgin with the words: *Maris Stella succure nobis* ('Star of the Sea, Assist us'). At nightfall each day, Columbus gathered his crew to salute their protectress and to sing *Salve Regina*. Back in Spain in 1493, he gave thanks for his safe return by visiting the monastery and shrine of Our Lady of Guadalupe, the celebrated Black Madonna, on the slope of the Sierra de Extremadura.

Some years later in 1521, Hernán Cortés – a native of Extremadura – confronted and defeated the Aztec empire of Moctezuma II. He had with him painted and sculpted images of the Virgin Mary, regarded by the Spaniards as their champion in time of conflict. A decade later, in 1531, a miraculous apparition of the Virgin Mary gave Mesoamericans their own Christian devotion and symbol: *la Virgen Morena* (the dark-skinned Virgin). In 1999 the Roman Catholic church officially proclaimed her the first and greatest evangelizer of the Americas.

According to traditional accounts, the Virgin chose to appear at the hill of Tepeyac, just north of Mexico City, to Juan Diego – an indigenous Nahuatl-speaker and Christian convert. She asked him to tell the bishop of Mexico, Juan de Zumárraga, to build a chapel in her honour. Juan Diego followed her instructions but was rebuffed. When he told the Virgin of his failure, she commanded him to seek a second meeting. Still unconvinced, Zumárraga asked for a sign that would confirm the Virgin's request. During their third encounter, the Virgin provided Juan Diego with the necessary

above
Image of Our Lady of Guadalupe, regarded as the mother of all Mexicans. In the technique of *popote*, dyed straws are stuck down one by one on to thick card. Mexico state, late 1980s. Ht 35 cm.

opposite
Carved figure of Our Lady of Guadalupe, patron saint of Mexico. Cow-horn has been heated, flattened in a clamp, cut out and painted. San Antonio de la Isla, Mexico state, early 1970s. Ht 8.5 cm.

proof. Readmitted to Zumárraga's presence, Juan Diego opened his *tilma* (mantle). Flowers, gathered in the midst of winter, cascaded to the floor. More importantly, imprinted on his mantle was the image of the Virgin of Guadalupe. All scepticism gone, Zumárraga ordered the construction of a small church at Tepeyac.

Over time, further building programmes have vastly enlarged this holy site to keep pace with the growing popularity of the Virgin of Guadalupe. When an epidemic struck Mexico City, her divine intercession led the civil and ecclesiastical authorities to adopt her in 1737 as patroness of the capital. In 1754, she was declared patroness and protectress of New Spain: a papal bull, issued by Pope Benedict XIV, fixed 12 December – the anniversary of her last appearance to Juan Diego – as her feast day. In 1895, she was crowned queen of Mexico, amidst great rejoicing. In 1910 and 1945, proclamations by Pius X and Pius XII named her celestial patron of Latin America and empress of the Americas. In 2002, Juan Diego was canonized by John Paul II. Today Our Lady of Guadalupe presides over the richest and most visited Catholic shrine in all the Americas.

Thousands of pages have been written about *la Virgen Morena* and her role within Mexico. Many authors have pointed out that Tepeyac, before the Spanish conquest, was already a place of worship. It has been suggested that the Christian shrine may have replaced an earlier one dedicated to Tonantzin, a female deity associated with motherhood and earth fertility. Some investigators, Stafford Poole included, maintain that the Christian shrine was actually built *c.* 1555–6. They remind us that the story of the apparition did not appear in print until 1648. Interestingly, Poole challenges the widely accepted idea that Our Lady of Guadalupe was beloved initially by the native population: 'Contrary to the common assertion that the apparitions brought millions of Indians to Christianity – a claim for which there is no evidence whatever – it was only in the last half of the eighteenth

left

Printed holy picture with Our Lady of Guadalupe and the Mexican flag. Inspired by the miraculous 16th-century image on Juan Diego's *tilma* (mantle), the Virgin of Tepeyac is traditionally shown wearing a garment adorned with stars. The moon is her pedestal, and an angel with outstretched wings raises her high above the clouds. Her hands are joined in prayer, and she is surrounded by rays of light. Mexico City, late 1980s. Ht 16.5 cm.

below

Glass bottle for holy water shaped like Our Lady of Guadalupe. Late 1980s. Ht 23 cm.

century that the devotion began to spread among indigenous people, perhaps as part of a planned campaign by the church.'

According to Poole and a number of historians, 'devotion to the Guadalupe of the apparitions was confined almost entirely to the *criollo* population of New Spain'. The seventeenth and eighteenth centuries were a time of repression and control by the Spanish Crown. The *criollos*, Creoles of Spanish parentage but American-born, felt increasingly deprived of advancement. Like the *mestizos* (Mexicans of mixed European and indigenous descent), the *criollos* became eager to establish their own cultural identity. Importantly for the story of Roman Catholicism, Our Lady of Guadalupe became the symbol that launched the independence movement of 1810. Miguel Hidalgo y Costillas, a parish priest, used her image as a banner to symbolize the revolutionary struggle. In 1821, when independence was finally granted, *la Virgen Morena* was the force that bound disparate classes and ethnic groups into one nation. In 1914, when Emiliano Zapata led his peasant army into Mexico City, his followers carried Guadalupan banners.

At the start of the twenty-first century, Our Lady of Guadalupe remains the most visible symbol of religious faith in Mexico. Her likeness is rendered with devotion in painted clay, embroidered cloth, tin, wood, horn, glass, shell and a host of other materials. Surrounded by rays of light, she looks out from household altars and from shrines in markets, bars and other public places. Her protection is sought by the drivers of buses and taxicabs, as well as by soldiers, prisoners and the police force. She is present on prayer sheets, T-shirts, fridge magnets, medallions, amulets, key rings, shopping bags and neighbourhood murals. Young men display her tattooed image with the word Lupe – her name in its diminutive and most affectionate form. Her followers have even seen her appear in street puddles, trees and spilt coffee grounds. An 'untouchable' institution, *la Virgen Morena* is the

opposite
Ceremonial *servilleta* (cloth) embroidered in cross-stitch by Reina Martínez González to honour Our Lady of Guadalupe. Alaxtitla Postectitla, Veracruz state, late 1980s. 88 x 81 cm.

overleaf
Reyna de México (Queen of Mexico) in the atrium of the basilica at Tepeyac, 1998. Photographer's painted backdrop with a three-dimensional image of Our Lady of Guadalupe surrounded by plastic flowers. Many pilgrims like to keep a photographic memento of their visit to her shrine.

mother of all Mexicans, seen now as the liberator of the poor and the disenfranchised. Although 'anti-apparitionists' may argue that the image on Juan Diego's *tilma* was painted by human hands, most Mexicans prefer the idea of a supernatural origin. As the distinguished writer Carlos Fuentes has said, when interviewed in July 2006 for the Chilean newspaper *El Mercurio*, the Virgin of Guadalupe 'is the only certain reality in Mexico. She is everything in which people really believe.' Mexico has other miraculous and beloved Virgins, but Our Lady of Guadalupe is the binding force that unites the nation.

Regarded as the holiest place in Mexico, la Villa de Guadalupe – her shrine at Tepeyac – draws visitors like a magnet. Pilgrims enter the basilica in their tens of thousands each year to pray, ask for favours and gaze up at Juan Diego's *tilma* as they are carried past it on a moving walkway. Outside, in the huge atrium, itinerant photographers set up painted backdrops featuring the Virgin of Guadalupe garlanded with flowers. The food market nearby offers sustenance to weary pilgrims; souvenirs are sold in vast quantities by official shops and street vendors. In mid November, groups of unpaid *pirotécnicos* (firework makers) gather in the atrium to offer up their finest work. In front of her basilica, they set up monumental cane constructions termed *castillos* (castles). As darkness descends and the touch-paper is lit, angels, crowns, bells, birds and smiling suns of coloured light spin like great Catherine wheels. At the apex of each *castillo*, vivid against the night sky, the Virgin of Guadalupe is revealed, accompanied by words such as *Reina de México* (Queen of Mexico) or *Madre de Dios* (Mother of God).

Her feast day on 12 December is a time of great rejoicing. Festivities begin on the preceding evening, with the arrival at the basilica of pilgrims, musicians and dance troupes from near and far. Groups of *conchero* dancers assemble in the atrium, where they will greet the rising sun. Organized along military lines, *conchero* dancers have a special affinity with the shrine

at Tepeyac. Wearing opulent costumes trimmed with sequins and gold braid, elaborate plumed headdresses and seed rattles tied around their ankles, they burn *copal* incense and dance in concentric circles, combining 'Aztec'-style rituals with devotion to *la Virgen Morena*.

Outside the capital, in towns and villages, ceremonies are held to honour Mexico's patron saint. The day begins at dawn with volleys of rockets, as the devout visit her image to sing *las mañanitas* (birthday greetings). Floral archways may be erected outside churches; decorative pathways of dyed sand or sawdust may be laid for worshippers to follow as they process through the streets with her image. In Papantla, Veracruz,

Male and female *conchero* dancers performing in the atrium of the basilica, 12 December 1985. The splendour of the pre-Hispanic world is evoked by their richly decorated garments, spectacular headdresses and plumed shields. Intense drumming and the rattling of seed pods attached to their ankles provide a rhythmic accompaniment. Performers also play a mandolin-like instrument made from the *concha* (carapace) of an armadillo.

mestizo children are dressed in indigenous clothing: small boys with painted moustaches and white calico clothing represent Juan Diego. In Cuetzalan and surrounding villages in the highlands of Puebla, Nahuatl-speakers perform a range of dances; churches in the region display enormous locally made wax candles with the delicacy of lace. In the evening, many celebrations culminate in fireworks and the burning of a *castillo*. Repeated year after year, this outpouring of devotion remains the most powerful example of the way that Roman Catholicism has been adopted and adapted on Mexican soil.

Group of *Matlachines* (also called *Matachines*) dancers from Zacatecas state performing in the atrium of the basilica, 12 December 1985. Holding gourd rattles, performers execute carefully choreographed dance steps accompanied by violin music and watched over by their *capitán* (captain).

Christmas Festivities

Todos los pastores
vamos a Belén
a adorar el niño
y a María también.

Y los gallos cantan
y el demonio llora,
porque ya nació
el rey de la gloria.

We are shepherds
going to Bethlehem
to adore the Christ-child
and Mary too.

The roosters crow
and the Devil weeps,
because the King of Kings
was born today.

Popular Christmas verses

In Mexico, Christmas is perceived not as a single day but as a season that runs from 16 December to the Feast of the Epiphany on 6 January. The ceremonial cycle closes with the Feast of the Purification of the Blessed Virgin on 2 February. As always, the makers of festive items start production long before the Christmas season arrives.

When the Capuchin friar, Francisco de Ajofrín, visited Mexico City in 1763, he saw 'a great market and colourful fair in the portals of the merchants'. The inhabitants of the capital came 'to look at and purchase nativity scenes' on Christmas Eve and Christmas Day. In 1897 *The Mexican Herald* published a description of festive stalls, seen on 16 December in the capital's *zócalo* (main square). On sale were variously shaped *piñatas* and 'figures of the holy pilgrims'. The writer was moved by this 'picturesque sight' or 'children's paradise', 'with its concourse of people, its cressets, bonfires, and heaps of pea-nuts, not to speak of the dazzling array of the objects for sale'. In modern-day Mexico City and commercial centres throughout Mexico, market vendors continue to offer celebrants a profusion of Christmas goods.

As in Europe, the Mexican nativity scene is central to the idea of Christmas. Although the Gospels devote just a few lines to the birth of Jesus, it has been celebrated by the Christian Church since the fourth century. It has also captured the imagination of countless artists. After the overthrow of the Aztec empire in 1521, ecclesiastical paintings and carved representations provided indigenous peoples with a visual account of Christ's origins. The church and former convent of San Bernardino, built

above
Angel of painted pottery, part of a group of figures from a Christmas nativity scene, mid 1980s (see overleaf). Ht 24 cm.

opposite
Devil of painted pottery made from an old mould in Tlaquepaque, Jalisco state, for a *nacimiento* (Christmas nativity scene). Mid 1970s. Ht 16 cm.

Christmas *tableau* of painted pottery from the Purépecha village of Ocumicho, Michoacán, mid 1970s. *Belenes* or *misterios* traditionally show just Joseph, the Virgin and baby Jesus. Joseph carries a lily. Ht 29.5 cm.

Nacimiento (Christmas nativity scene) of painted pottery, made by the Aguilar family in Ocotlán de Morelos, Oaxaca state, mid 1980s. Ht (white-robed angel) 24 cm.

after 1535 near Mexico City in Xochimilco, was one of the first Franciscan foundations of New Spain. The splendid Renaissance *retablo* (monumental altarpiece) incorporated fine paintings showing the Annunciation and Adoration of the Shepherds. San Miguel Arcángel in Huejotzingo, Puebla, is another former Franciscan convent with an early *retablo*. Executed *c.* 1585 in Mannerist style, it shows the Adoration of the Shepherds, the Adoration of the Kings and other key scenes from Christ's life.

The creation of the first Christmas *crèche* involving people and animals has been attributed to St Francis of Assisi, founder of the Franciscan order. In 1223, in the Italian town of Greccio, he expanded his Christmas sermon with a *tableau vivant* of the Holy Family. Inspired by earlier liturgical ceremonies, St Francis set up a simple manger with a living ox and ass. Local people may have taken the roles of Mary, Joseph and the shepherds. Franciscan friars, after their arrival in New Spain, habitually staged 'mysteries' or nativity plays; these were accompanied by hymns praising the Divine Infant.

Franciscans also encouraged the diffusion of imported Neapolitan and Spanish *crèches* of wood, terracotta and wax. Carved ivory figures, commissioned in the Orient, reached Acapulco on great galleons from Manila. Soon, however, popular piety found its own form of expression in New Spain. Artisans used clay, wax, silver and wood – painted or gilded – to represent the Holy Family in the stable. Initially called *belenes* (Bethlehems) or *misterios* (mysteries), they conveyed the central mystery of the Incarnation and the origin of Christianity. Over time, these simple scenes grew into elaborate installations, replete with choirs of angels and shepherds watching their flocks. The Three Magi, sumptuously attired, were shown riding a horse, a camel and an elephant to symbolize their places of origin.

below
One of the Three Kings, part of a group of painted pottery figures from a Christmas nativity scene, mid 1980s (opposite). Ht 22.5 cm.

opposite
Tableau of painted wood with nativity figures from Oaxaca state, mid 1980s. 31.5 x 35 cm.

left
Woman grinding maize on a *metate*. This painted pottery figurine was made in Tlaquepaque, Jalisco state, mid 1980s, for a nativity scene. Ht 9 cm.

During the nineteenth century, with the rise of nationalism, nativity scenes took on a Mexican identity. In Mexican homes, the Holy Family was accompanied by figures from working-class life. These included market vendors, butchers, *tortilla* makers and agave-harvesters, also *campesinos* and *campesinas* (peasants) wearing regional dress. Devils too made an appearance, with horns and tails, to represent the evils of temptation. These large and sometimes disparate casts of characters were often displayed in simulated landscapes that incorporated not just elephants and camels but turkeys, writhing serpents, village pumps, cabbages, *nopales* (prickly pears) and *maguey* plants.

Frederick Starr, the North American ethnographer, visited Mexico in the late 1890s to make a collection of artefacts for the British Folk-Lore Society. While on his travels, he purchased several nativity figures from Toluca and Guadalajara, made of wax and clay respectively. Although the 'scene of the child in the manger' was always represented, this was sometimes 'but a small item', he noted. Starr was struck by the incongruous style and scale of some figures and scenic elements. Although 'these may be tastefully and handsomely arranged', he observed, 'they are often quite grotesque from lack of attention to consistency and proportion'.

Starr has left us an evocative description of a household *nacimiento* in the town of Morelia:

> … the whole of one side of the room was occupied with a landscape composed of rockwork and representing hills, valleys, etc. At one side was a train of pack-mules and an attack of bandits: at its side and the central piece was the Garden of Eden from which the first pair were being driven out by an angel with a flaming sword. Adam and Eve were being driven forth into a desert. Next to this, however, was another group representing the Expulsion: but this time the race-parents are going forth into a scene of festivity – farms, cows being milked, crops being gathered, old women contentedly smoking, a band of music playing, and a company of young people gaily dancing.

After the Mexican Revolution, the search for Mexico's cultural roots refocused interest on the *nacimiento*. Today the sale of brightly painted nativity figurines, many made from old moulds, remains an important source of revenue for families in ceramic centres such as Tlaquepaque in the state of Jalisco. In Metepec, meanwhile, ceramic artists like Tiburcio Soteno regularly receive commissions to make life-size representations of the Holy Family and their entourage for churches, shops and hotels.

In recent years, a succession of *concursos* (contests) has further invigorated the making of nativity figures. Traditional and non-traditional materials have included not just clay and wax but also wood, paper, glass, tin, lead, copper, bone, horn, cloth, palm, *totomoxtle* (maize husks), *panicua* (wheat straw), gourds, seeds, plaited vanilla, *chilte* (gum), *alfeñique* (sugar paste) and *cacao* (chocolate). In 1985 the British Museum acquired a group

opposite
Mexican-style *nacimiento* (Christmas nativity scene) made from *dulce de pepita* (sweetened pumpkin-seed paste). Arranged on a wooden board, figures include the Holy Family, sheep, birds, farmers, *nopales* (prickly pears) and *magueyes* (agaves). Malinaltenango, Mexico state, mid 1980s. Ht 16.5 cm, width 46 cm, depth 57 cm.

of prize-winning Mexican *nacimientos*. Included was an ambitious three-dimensional scene made in Malinaltenango, state of Mexico, from *dulce de pepita* (sweetened pumpkin-seed paste). Visitors to Oaxaca City on 23 December are certain to see other unusual *nacimientos*. Displayed in the main plazas are artworks made from enormous carved radishes and *tableaux* of 'everlasting' flowers from San Antonino Castillo Velasco. Both categories invariably include nativity scenes.

Many commentators have sought to explain why Mexicans of every social class continue to show such loyalty to the traditional *nacimiento*, even regarding it as something uniquely Mexican. According to the Tabascan poet Carlos Pellicer (1899–1977), Mexicans delight in constructing vast and ingenious nativity scenes because they have a strong sense of theatre. A keen collector of *nacimientos*, Pellicer enjoyed setting up highly elaborate Christmas installations of his own – sometimes with the addition of lighting, flowers, foliage, music and verse. He described these acts of creation as 'a profound, humble expression of faith'. As Margarita de Orellana makes clear in her essay *Epifanías artesanales* ('An Epiphany in Crafts'), the Christmas *crèche* celebrates the arrival of God as a child in the profane world. For Roman Catholics, it proclaims the birth of God Himself. Each year, in countless homes, newly purchased nativity figures join older ones. Spanish moss carpets the surrounding landscape. Mirrors serve as lakes, rivers of silver paper run between painted pottery bridges, and cotton-wool balls become heavenly clouds.

Although the *piñata* is now a feature of children's parties throughout the year, it has a long-standing association with Christmas. Various theories have been put forward to explain the origin of the *piñata* and its adoption in Mexico, but few sources offer reliable information. Perhaps its antecedents lie in Italy, where the word *pignatta* refers to an earthenware cooking pot. During the Italian game of *la pentolaccia*, a clay pot is filled

opposite
Devil of painted pottery made from an old mould in Tlaquepaque, Jalisco state, 1980s, for a *nacimiento* (Christmas nativity scene). Ht 23 cm.

with sweets and gifts, then suspended by a rope; contestants wearing a blindfold must hit the pot with a stick to bring it down. In an alternative version of this game, the pot may be filled with water to drench the participants. From Italy the custom may have passed via Spain to New Spain. The former Augustinian convent of San Agustín Acolman, in the state of Mexico, played a crucial role in the spread of Christian teachings, and according to local lore, the *piñata* was first introduced here – within the context of Christmas – by the convent's founders.

Until recently, most Mexican *piñatas* were fired ceramic pots covered with colourful layers of cut paper. The form often made symbolic reference to Christianity. The seven deadly sins were represented by a star with seven points. We are told by contemporary commentators Fernando Henao Giraldo and Everardo Gordillo Estrada that this style of *piñata* represented the struggle of the believer: the stick symbolizes our religious faith as we battle against our evil passions. These same authors remind us that the *piñata* was meant for adults as well as children. They quote an account, published in 1989, by a nameless inhabitant of Mexico City. Looking back on his youth, the anonymous writer recalled '*piñatas* for adults as well as young folk. When the adults tried to break their *piñata*, we were not allowed to join in because we were too young ... Imagine my astonishment when one broke – everyone rushed forward, and emerged totally black ... someone had filled it with black *zapote* fruits and ashes.'

Frederick Starr penned a useful description of Mexican *piñatas* in the 1890s, when makers were already offering a surprising range of styles: '*Piñatas* are of all sizes and degrees of elaborateness in decoration. They are made to represent flowers, pineapples and other fruits, human beings, naguals, quadrupeds, birds, fish, devil on bicycle, devils, lyre, boat, cornucopia, etc. While usually filled with bonbons, pea-nuts, fruit, etc.,

they may contain a quite different filling. Water and ashes are not uncommon contents.' Like the anonymous writer already quoted, Starr mentioned a *piñata* filled with fleshy black *zapotes*, which was offered by the Archbishop of Morelia to his guests before Christmas. According to Starr, 'The garments of men, women and children who scrambled for the contents of the *piñata* were in a fearful state.'

Modern *piñata*-makers prefer to offer pleasant surprises aimed at children. Their range has expanded in recent years to include airplanes and space rockets, together with representations of Snow White, Batman and Spiderman. For reasons of convenience and safety, papier mâché has largely replaced the ceramic pots that once threatened bystanders with sharp, flying sherds. Despite these changes, however, the rhyme remains the same: *'Dale, dale, dale, no pierdes el tino. Porque si lo pierdes, pierdes el camino …'* (Hit it, hit it, hit it, do not lose your aim. Because if you lose it, you will lose your way …'). Children still look up eagerly as the *piñata* is dangled tantalizingly above them on a rope. One by one, participants accept the blindfold and strike out with a stout stick. When the *piñata* finally explodes, it sends forth a cascade of seasonal fruits, sugarcane, nuts, confetti and small presents.

Christmas Day is preceded by nine *posadas* – translatable, literally, as 'lodgings'. From 16 to 24 December, in urban neighbourhoods and rural communities, traditionally minded families and groups of worshippers re-enact the nativity story of Mary and Joseph as they search for shelter on their way to Bethlehem. Children play key roles, often impersonating angels or shepherds and wearing appropriate costumes. As the procession proceeds from door to door, the pilgrims carry lighted candles and sing verses. 'In heaven's name, I beg for shelter', implores Joseph, 'My wife tonight can go no further'. Residents then sing their refusal: 'No inn is this, Be gone from hence. You may be thieves, I dare not open.' When the pilgrims are finally admitted, they make their way to the *crèche* to kneel and pray. Participants

opposite
Painted pottery candelabrum in the form of a 'tree of life' showing a nativity scene. Small figures are suspended on wires. Made by the Castillo family in Izúcar de Matamoros, Puebla state, mid 1980s.
Ht 45 cm.

below
Banner of cut tissue paper showing people gathered beneath a *piñata* with the words *Feliz Navidad* (Happy Christmas). Made in 1993 by Ernesto Vivanco of San Salvador Huixcolotla, Puebla state.
Ht 64.5 cm.

are usually invited to eat and drink, and each party culminates in the breaking of a *piñata*.

The ninth *posada* takes place on *Nochebuena* (Christmas Eve) and commemorates the birth of the Saviour. The Holy Family is welcomed with great rejoicing:

Dichosa la casa	Blessed is the house
Que abriga este día	That shelters this day
A la Virgen pura	The Virgin Pure
La hermosa María.	The beautiful Maria.

In many homes, the manger at the centre of the nativity scene remains empty until 24 December. As Jesus is welcomed into the world, the figure of the *Niño Dios* (Christ-child) is passed round, embraced by those present,

Pictures painted on bark paper in Nahua villages such as Ameyaltepec, Guerrero state, often display lively scenes inspired by village life. The same painting style has been used for this decorative pair of carved and painted wooden fish. Both were made in Guerrero state in the mid 1980s for a contest of *nacimientos* (nativity scenes).

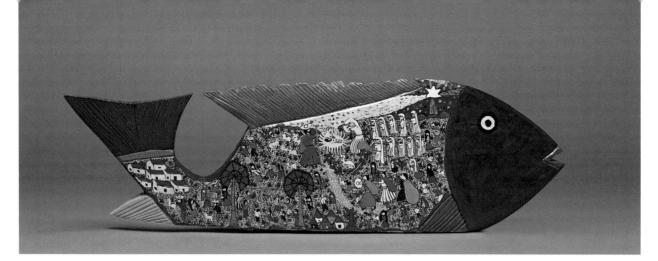

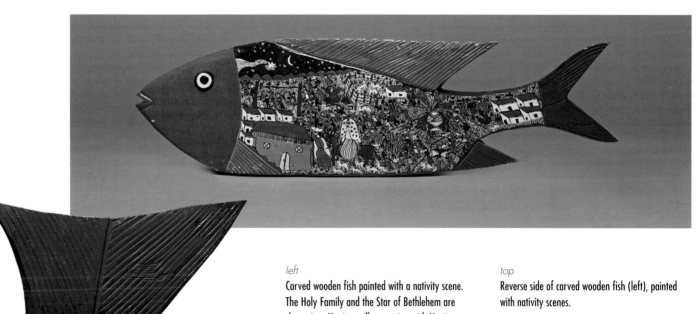

left
Carved wooden fish painted with a nativity scene.
The Holy Family and the Star of Bethlehem are
shown in a Mexican village setting with Mexican
vegetation. White-garbed shepherdesses and three
'Wise Women' approach the crib to adore the
Christ-child. 16.5 x 56 cm.

top
Reverse side of carved wooden fish (left), painted
with nativity scenes.

above
Carved wooden fish painted with a nativity scene:
Joseph asks for lodging (*posada*) while Mary, clothed
in white, sits on a horse. In Mexico, from 16 to 24
December, people stage *posadas* that re-enact the
Christmas story of Mary and Joseph as they search
for shelter on their way to Bethlehem. 15 x 52.5 cm.

Performer rehearsing the role of Asmodeo, companion to Luzbel (Lucifer) in the *pastorela* (Christmas dance-drama), 1988. He wears a lacquered wooden mask carved by Victoriano Salgado Morales. The performance takes place each year on 24 December in the Barrio de La Magdalena, Uruapan, Michoacán state.

and placed in the crib where he will remain until 6 January, or even 2 February, when the nativity scene is dismantled.

Some families celebrate Christmas Eve by going to Midnight Mass. Others stay at home to consume a celebratory dinner. Popular foods include turkey, *tamales* (steamed cakes of cornmeal dough), *bacalao* (salt cod) and *buñuelos* (crisp pancakes). *Romeritos en revoltijo* is a dish made from dried shrimps, *nopales*, potatoes and *romeritos* (small green leaves akin to rosemary); ingredients are cooked in a rich *mole* sauce. Christmas *ponche* (punch) is prepared with alcohol, sugar, seasonal fruits, cinnamon and cloves.

In rural communities, many villagers still perform open-air dance-dramas known as *pastorelas*, or shepherds' nativity plays. These are versions of the miracle plays that were introduced into New Spain by *la Compañía de Jesús* (Society of Jesus) and other religious orders. Watched by neighbours and visitors from surrounding villages, adults and children take the roles of shepherds and shepherdesses, angels, devils and *ermitaños* (hermits). As the shepherds travel to Bethlehem to adore baby Jesus, their way is continually blocked by Luzbel (Lucifer) and his aides, the capital sins. Eventually the forces of virtue triumph. Clothed in white to symbolize their purity, archangels Michael, Gabriel and Raphael wield their swords and carry the day.

Carved wooden dance-mask from Guanajuato state, pre-1984. The wearer impersonates the devil during the *pastorela* (Christmas dance-drama). Reptiles, insects such as scorpions, and other creatures (painted and carved) are traditionally represented on the face to inspire fear. Ht 28 cm.

The dialogue and the details of the story, which vary from place to place, are close in spirit to the *pastorelas* that were printed during the nineteenth century by popular publishing houses like that of Antonio Vanegas Arroyo. The tradition remains especially strong in the state of Michoacán. On 24 December in Uruapan, in the Barrio de La Magdalena, Luzbel wears a red veil over his face and a red cape. His companions – Asmodeo, Astucia and Satanás – wear lacquered wooden masks carved by Victoriano Salgado Morales or his son Martín. In the Purépecha-speaking village of Ocumicho, on 24 and 25 December, heavy veils cover the faces of Luzbel and his followers: as the hours pass, they pace threateningly backwards and forwards outside the church, declaiming lines that assert their evil intent. Masked hermits and devils, sometimes played by small boys, act as clowns and buffoons.

During many of these performances, considerable emphasis is

given to the tragic potential of Luzbel's predicament. Carlos F. Márquez, in the Michoacán edition of *La Jornada* for 26 December 2005, quotes some of the lyrical and powerful lines spoken by Luzbel:

> *¡Ay, Ay!, yo era el ángel más bello del cielo / y por mi envidia / fui arrojado al profundo infierno / donde hoy me encuentro.*
>
> *¡Ay qué tormento! / malaya será mi suerte / yo tan bello en mi ser / cuando los seres de la Tierra estaban en mi poder.*
>
> Woe! Woe! I was once the most beautiful angel in heaven / but because of my envy / I was cast into deepest hell / where I now reside.
>
> What anguish! How accursed my fate! / How beautiful I once was / when the creatures of the Earth were under my dominion.

The Feast of the Epiphany on 6 January commemorates the arrival of the Three Magi bearing gifts for the infant Jesus. Once *el día de los Santos Reyes* (Day of the Holy Kings) was when urban children traditionally received their presents. On 5 January, they would place their shoes in readiness near the manger, with its precious figure of the Christ-child. In recent decades, however, the importance of 6 January has been weakened by the growing popularity of Santa Claus, snow-laden Christmas trees, and the idea of gift-giving on 25 December. Both traditions can be observed in tandem in Mexico City. As reported on 3 January 2007 in *El Sol de México*, itinerant photographers set up their eye-catching installations each year on Avenida Hidalgo. Santa Claus rules during the run-up to Christmas. After 26 December, however, his reindeer are replaced by elephants, camels and horses as the Three Kings take over for their big day on 6 January.

Despite changing times, the Feast of the Epiphany is still associated with the eating of a *rosca de reyes*. This is a ring-shaped cake, filled with dried fruits. Importantly, it contains a hidden figure of the Christ-child. According to long-standing custom, the finder of this tiny doll – once made

opposite
Dance-mask of black-lacquered wood carved by Victoriano Salgado Morales, *c.* 1989. He has added real teeth and horns. The wearer takes the role of Satanás (Satan) during the *pastorela* (Christmas dance-drama) performed each year on 24 December in the Barrio de La Magdalena, Uruapan, Michoacán state. Ht 26.5 cm.

The *pastorela* is performed on Christmas Day each year by the Purépecha villagers of Ocumicho, Michoacán. Heavy veils cover the faces of Luzbel (Lucifer) and his followers, giving them a sinister appearance. 1988.

from porcelain, but now increasingly of plastic – should host a party on 2 February.

With the festival of the Purification of the Blessed Virgin, also known as *la candelaria* (Candlemas), the Christmas cycle ends. Families go to church: candles are blessed, and Jesus is symbolically 'presented'. First, however, he will need new clothes. In shops and markets across Mexico, the same sign appears: *Aquí se visten Niños Dios* (Baby Jesuses dressed here). After the presentation in church, people gather at home to pay homage to the Christ-child and to celebrate the first forty days of his life. Placed in a sitting position and wearing his new apparel, the figure of the *Niño Dios* and his mother Mary are venerated with flowers, prayers, music and feasting.

Purépecha women wearing lavishly decorated hats take the role of shepherdesses during the Christmas *pastorela* in Ocumicho, Michoacán, 1988. Boys often have a comic role: while some dress as masked devils, others don wooden masks and pointed hats to perform as *ermitaños* (hermits).

Carnival and Saints' Days: Masquerades

Miércoles de Ceniza
Se despiden los amantes
Y hasta el Sábado de Gloria
Vuelven a lo que eran antes.

On Ash Wednesday
Lovers take leave of love
Until the Saturday of Glory
When they love again.

*Otomí verse for Carnival
(heard in Huixquilucan by Frances Toor)*

Celebrated in February or March, the pre-Lenten festival of Carnival – literally a 'giving up' or 'farewell' to meat (*carnem levare* or *carne vale*) – originated in Italy. As this humorous verse suggests, its meaning extends to other sensual pleasures. Timothy Hyman, a contemporary artist and writer, succinctly describes the ethos of Carnival in his essay, *A Carnival Sense of the World*:

> While Carnival is first recorded as a pre-Lenten feast only in the Middle Ages, most anthropologists locate its origins much earlier, in pre-Christian ritual and especially in the Saturnalia – the period of licence and excess, when inversion of rank was a central theme. Slaves were set free and given the right to ridicule their masters; a mock-king was elected; the lost Golden Age of the deposed god Saturn was temporarily reinstated. Affinities to more distant traditions – the Jewish Purim or the Indian Holi – suggest a structure deeply implanted in mankind: a moment each year when for a few days the laughter of disorder comes out from the margins and assumes centre-stage.

The first documented references to the celebration of *carnaval* in New Spain date from the eighteenth

above
Dancers performing as *españoles* (Spaniards) in 1992 during Carnival celebrations in Tlaxcala state. Male dancers wear finely carved masks (see pp. 80–1). Although women now take part, 'female' partners were formerly played by men wearing female masks.

opposite
Dance-mask of painted wood from Guerrero state, early 1970s, representing an Aztec 'eagle-warrior' with a plumed headdress. Numerous dances in Mexico re-enact the Spanish Conquest. Ht 48 cm.

Masked Nahua performer in the mountain village of Totoltepec, Guerrero state, in 1978. He takes the role of the *tigre* (tiger) during the *danza de los tlacololeros* (farmers) – one of several dances linked with agriculture. Similar masquerades would once have featured jaguars or ocelots.

opposite
Nahua dance-mask of painted wood representing a *tigre* (tiger), from Guerrero state, early 1970s. It is equipped with real teeth, bristles for whiskers, and mirrors for eyes. Masks are usually carved from a soft, light wood such as *tzompantle* or *colorin* ('coral' tree). Ht 25.5 cm.

century. Barbara Mauldin, editor of *¡Carnival!*, notes in her essay *Ritual and Play* that official complaints were filed about the rowdiness of festivities and the scandalousness of some masqueraders. Indigenous populations were presumably excluded from these initially urban festivities. Independence from Spain, granted in 1821, gave greater freedom to all social classes. During the colonial period, strict laws regarding dress had reinforced the 'caste' system and regulated the use of finery. After 1821, however, these rulings became obsolete. By the late nineteenth century, *carnaval* had become popular with indigenous populations and with the ever-growing *mestizo* class (Mexicans of mixed European and indigenous descent). Participants were able to make fun of sumptuously dressed Europeans, wealthy landowners and other authority figures. Today urban celebrations for *carnaval* are usually flamboyant. In the port of Veracruz, the festival starts nine days before Lent. Promoted as the most spectacular Carnival outside Brazil, it opens as many Mexican Carnivals do with the burning of a figure called *El Mal Humor* (Bad Humour). After his demise, fancifully masked revellers join costumed drag queens and scantily clad women for lavishly choreographed parades.

In rural communities, by contrast, *carnaval* has important links with agriculture. Where subsistence farmers need to wrest a living from the soil, festivities mark the transition from the dry season to the rainy season. Village celebrations for *carnaval* incorporate a

wide range of creatures and characters from the Old and New Worlds. Dancers often wear wooden masks to impersonate bulls, monkeys, dogs, goats, Death, devils, angels, *viejos* (old men), farmers and fishermen. The *tigre* (tiger) appears in a number of masquerades that would once have featured jaguars or ocelots. In many versions, the *tigre* is chased by angry farmers anxious to protect their crops. At the end of the day, the *tigre* is caught and killed.

The dance-cycle known as *moros y cristianos* (Moors and Christians) has many regional variations. These involve the re-enactment of battles that took place long ago on Spanish soil. *Conquista* (Conquest) dances similarly commemorate the subjugation of Mexico's indigenous population by Spanish soldiers: the Aztec ruler Moctezuma loses his treasures and his empire, but is given the Christian cross in exchange. During Carnival festivities in the state of Morelos, *chinelo* dancers wear long velvet robes and lightweight wire-mesh masks with painted features: beard, moustache and eyebrows are made from *ixtle* (agave fibre). *Chinelo* hats, tall and richly decorated, often display flashing lights. Although the origin of this dance remains unclear, *chinelos* may represent Moors. In Atenco, Los Reyes and other communities bordering Mexico City, Carnival celebrations evoke the pre-Revolutionary world of the great *haciendas*. Wearing magnificently embroidered clothing and elegant masks of wax-covered cloth, participants enjoy ridiculing the pretentions of nineteenth-century landowners. The humour of reversal is also central to festivities in the Puebla highlands: young Otomí men in San Pablito borrow the gala clothing of female relatives and dress as 'women'. Although masks are not used,

opposite

Dance-mask of painted wood representing a devil. The maker has used animal hair and real horns. Glass marbles are embedded in the eye sockets, and carved serpents surround the face. Probably from Guanajuato state, pre-1984. Ht 30.5 cm.

below

La danza de los moros (Dance of the Moors) in painted pottery from the Purépecha village of Ocumicho, Michoacán, early 1970s. The dancers' unmasked faces are partially covered by a kerchief. Their tall hats display rosettes and their garments are trimmed with coloured ribbons and braid. Ht 28 cm.

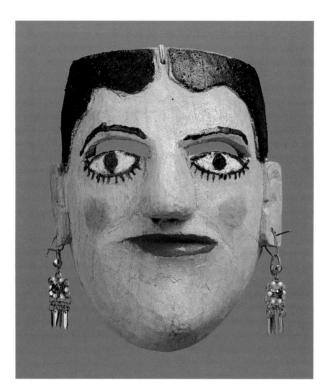

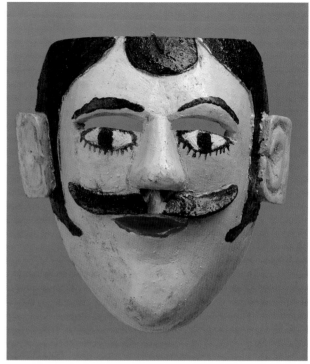

the identity of dancers is concealed by scarves and dark glasses. These indicate, as masks do, that the wearer is no longer his everyday self: he has undergone a transformation for the duration of the festive period.

Carnival in the town of Huejotzingo, Puebla, attracts a vast audience. Over several days, hundreds of elaborately dressed performers re-enact the defeat of French imperial troops by Mexican forces on 5 May 1862. Battalions of French *Zuavos*, *Zapadores* (Sappers) and *Zacapoaxtlas* (heroic Mexican fighters from the Puebla highlands) mingle with groups of *Indios Serranos* (impoverished mountain people) and *Apaches* wearing colourful feathered costumes. Masks of moulded leather display heavy beards of animal or human hair. As the battle climaxes on the final day, the smell of

above

Female and male dance-masks of painted wood for *la danza de los huehues* (literally 'old ones'). They were carved by Salvador Cortés Pérez in the Totonac village of Lázaro Cárdenas near Chumatlán, Veracruz state, in the late 1980s. The dancers perform in pairs, with men taking both male and 'female' roles. Ht (left) 18.5 cm, (right) 17 cm.

opposite

Dance-mask of painted wood representing a skull. The character of *la muerte* (Death) participates in numerous dances with allegorical themes, and is frequently partnered by the Devil. Provenance unknown, pre-1989. Ht 22 cm.

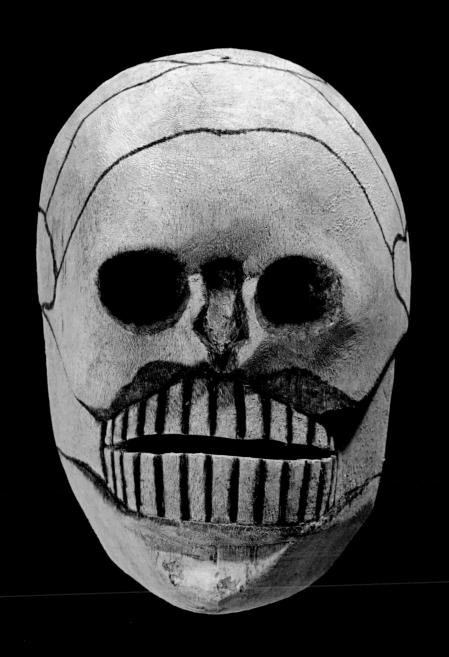

above
Male Carnival dancers in 1986 in the Otomí (nyûhû)
village of San Pablito, Puebla state.

opposite (left to right)
Figures made in Veracruz state, 1980s.

Performer from *la danza de los Matlachines* (or *Matachines*), Zacatecas state.
Ht 38.5 cm.

Carnival performer wearing the feathered costume of an *Apache* in Huejotzingo,
Puebla state. Ht 48.5 cm.

Zuavo (soldier in the French regiment) wearing a Carnival mask of leather
in Huejotzingo, Puebla state. Ht 37.5 cm.

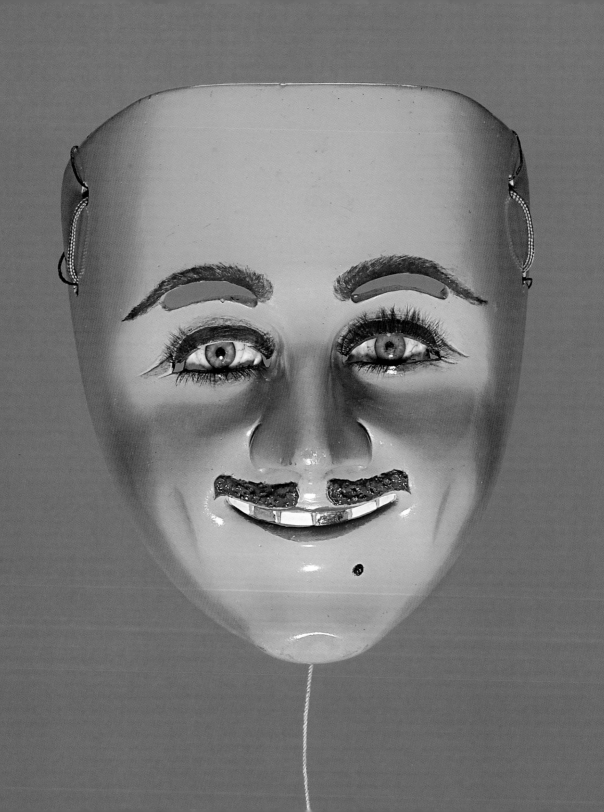

left
Pedro Amador Reyes Juárez making Carnival masks in 1996 in his workshop in Tlatempan, San Pedro Apetatitlán, Tlaxcala state. Measurements are very important, as masks are commissioned and carefully made to fit each wearer. The late don Pedro not only created exquisite masks; he was also a sculptor and an eminent *santero* (saint-carver).

gunpowder fills the air. Taking place simultaneously is the story of Agustín Lorenzo, a dashing bandit, who elopes with the daughter of a rich landowner. Before the wedding's completion, Lorenzo is captured and killed.

Tlaxcala is a small state, yet *carnaval* is celebrated there with visual splendour in approximately thirty-eight towns and villages. The forty days that follow *mardi gras* are meant to be days of abstinence, but Tlaxcalan masquerades often continue well into the Lenten period. They reflect shared hopes for the success of the approaching planting season; participation is a serious and costly undertaking. Dances and costumes vary from place to place, but masks – of painted and gessoed wood – are similar. Commissioned locally or in Puebla City, these feature imported glass eyes and artificial eyelashes. Some masks are fitted with a secret spring: when the wearer pulls a string, movable eyelids flutter flirtatiously.

opposite
Beautifully finished wooden dance-mask with glass eyes and eyelashes of real hair, made before 1980 in Tlaxcala or Puebla state for the Tlaxcala Carnival. When the performer pulls the string, the eyelids close. Ht (approx.) 20 cm.

Dancer's headdress of painted wood with feathers, mirrors, paper rosettes and hanging ribbons. Probably made in Guerrero state, early 1970s. Ht (headdress) 17 cm.

To the north of Tlaxcala City, dancers termed *catrines* (dandies) wear a tuxedo or frock coat, gloves and a top hat. Many hold up large umbrellas. This custom, as the ethnographer Ruth D. Lechuga has noted, is a rain-petitioning ceremony. Dancers perform in pairs: although 'female' partners were formerly played by masked men, women now take part in increasing numbers. In the south of the state, masqueraders wear ostrich-plumed headdresses with sequined and embroidered capes. Known as *charros*, they impersonate wealthy ranchers and carry long whips: when used in combat during *la danza de la culebra* (Dance of the Snake), these make a cracking sound like thunder. Snakes, the word dancers use for their whips, are symbolically linked with water in

above and left
Carnival celebrations in Tlaxcala state in 1992. Performers dress as *hacienda*-owners, and costumes are elaborate and extremely costly. *Charros* wear beautifully finished masks and richly embroidered capes. The best headdresses display 48 ostrich feathers. Dancers often learn the dance steps as small boys. Performances by women are a recent innovation.

opposite
Large painted wooden dance-belt representing
a horse from the Mixtec village of Pinotepa de
Don Luis, Oaxaca, late 1980s. A white horse is
traditionally worn by Santiago (St James) during
Conquista (Conquest) dances. Ht 54.5 cm.

Mexico. Large towns have several groups of dancers. Each group, with accompanying musicians, initially goes from house to house accepting donations. In the late afternoon, groups converge on the main square. In Amaxac de Guerrero, on the last day of festivities, hundreds of *catrines* gather in vast formations. Joining in the fun are masqueraders wearing commercially made rubber masks: these enable them to impersonate and mock unpopular politicians.

Saints' days are celebrated throughout Mexico. After the Conquest, each village and city *barrio* (neighbourhood) was assigned a patron saint. Venerated by the community as a special protector and spiritual intercessor, the saint is carried at the head of a procession. Often the occasion is marked by dances in the church atrium and surrounding streets. Although these dances may also be performed during *carnaval*, there is less emphasis during saints' days on comedy and misrule. Santiago Apóstol (St James the Apostle) is honoured on 25 July. He is represented in several dances commemorating the triumph of Christianity in Spain and New Spain. The dancer who plays Santiago usually wears a white-painted wooden horse at his waist. In Apaxtla, Guerrero, dancers perform *las tres potencias* (the Three Powers) for *la Virgen de la Candelaria* on 2 February. During this 'morality' pageant, which represents the battle between good and evil, the Soul struggles against Death and the Devil. On 20 January in Chiapa de Corzo, Chiapas state, celebrants don headdresses of *ixtle* (agave fibre) and finely carved masks to pay homage to San Sebastián. Their dance, *los Parachicos*, is said to commemorate the miraculous recovery of a sick boy in colonial times after the intervention of St Sebastian.

In addition to the Christian cycle of festivities, Mexicans everywhere celebrate their national Independence Day on 16 September. The town of Teloloapan, Guerrero, hosts a spectacular festival: *La mojiganga de los diablos* (the Mummery of Devils). Young men, dressed in long protective

Finely carved and painted dance-mask of wood from Chiapa de Corzo, Chiapas state, pre-1984. It has European features, glass eyes and a headdress of *ixtle* (agave fibre). On 20 January, in honour of St Sebastian, elegantly dressed dancers perform as *parachicos*. Translated literally, *para chico* means 'for the boy'. This dance is thought to commemorate the recovery of a sick boy in colonial times. Ht 31 cm.

opposite
Mask of painted wood with horns for *la mojiganga de los diablos* (Mummery of Devils). This event, which takes place in Teloloapan, Guerrero state, celebrates Mexican independence from Spain. Made by Fidel de la Puente in the mid 1970s, it has a flap of animal hide that hangs down the wearer's back. Ht 56 cm.

overcoats, wear enormous devil masks with fangs and horns; they also carry thickly plaited ropes as for a battle. Prizes are awarded by a jury for performance and appearance. Whatever the event being celebrated in Mexico, the essential impulse is positive and regenerative. This is especially true of Christian feast days – the most important events in the annual calendar – when high spirits and revelry are combined with a deep respect for spiritual beliefs and cultural values.

Holy Week: La Semana Santa

El sol se vistió de luto,
La luna se enterneció,
Las piedras vertieron sangre
Cuando Jesús expiró.

The sun was clothed in mourning,
The moon was moved to pity,
The stones shed blood
When Jesus expired.

Verse from a popular hymn

The crucifixion, burial and resurrection of Jesus Christ are central to the Christian faith; and they are commemorated each year in Mexico, as they have been since the spiritual Conquest that followed the fall of Tenochtitlan in 1521. Crosses and crucifixes, the symbols of Christ's martyrdom, were first introduced by the Franciscan order of missionary friars. Their Jesus was a loving and merciful saviour: unlike pre-Hispanic gods who required human blood, Jesus shed his own blood to redeem the world.

Indian compliance was complex, however. As the historian Charles Gibson has noted in his book, *The Aztecs under Spanish Rule*, 'The symbol of the crucifixion was accepted, but with an exaggerated concern for the details of an act of sacrifice.' Many friars were aware, even at the time of the conversion, that the martyrdom of Christ and of saints such as San Sebastián closely paralleled pre-Christian blood sacrifice. In both religious contexts, sacrifice engendered regeneration and rebirth. Nor was the cross an alien concept. Before the Conquest, cross-like forms were seen as a 'world tree' or cosmic symbol. The pre-Hispanic universe, considered vertically, incorporated thirteen celestial planes, our own terrestrial level, and nine planes of the underworld. Considered horizontally, the universe was determined by the four cardinal directions. A fifth cardinal point, the *axis mundi*, was the central tree that pierced the vertical layers of the universe and linked the heavens with the underworld. According to colonial sources, the Christian cross was enthusiastically received in New Spain. During the sixteenth and early seventeenth centuries, magnificent

above
Priest of painted pottery from Metepec, Mexico state, part of a funeral group, late 1980s (see p. 125). Ht 16 cm.

opposite
Christ on the cross: figure of lacquered wood made in the Nahua village of Temalacatzingo, Guerrero state, mid 1980s. Ht 39 cm.

Cristos de caña were venerated. Modelled by indigenous sculptors from maize paste and maize-stalk sections, these polychromed crosses showed Christ in agony on the cross. This method of construction had previously been used in regions such as Michoacán to make deity figures. Because *Cristos de caña* weighed comparatively little, they were easily carried during religious processions.

The sanctuary of Our Lord of Chalma, in the state of Mexico, is a shrine dedicated to Jesus Christ crucified. According to popular belief, an apparition of Jesus on the cross occurred in 1539. It was reportedly seen by local villagers in a cave where the pre-Christian god Oztoteotl had once been worshipped. The 'Black Christ of Chalma' is represented by a wooden sculpture of a dark-skinned Jesus, dead and bleeding from his wounds. Renowned as the 'patron of difficult causes', Our Lord of Chalma is visited each year by tens of thousands of pilgrims. Termed *chalmeros*, pilgrims often dance for many hours at his shrine. Nearby grows an ancient *ahuehuete* tree: from its branches hang crutches, clothing and locks of hair. These offerings give thanks for miracles already granted or serve as petitions in times of need.

It has been suggested by some anthropologists and historians that the conquered and oppressed peoples of Mesoamerica were able to identify in a very direct way with the crucified Christ. Powerful, contorted images of Christ's pain and humiliation may have been perceived as representations of Indian suffering. Because the crucifix embodies Christ's passage through birth and death to miraculous resurrection, it also paralleled pre-Conquest beliefs in a cosmic struggle. Christ, regarded by Christians as the 'Light of the World', had much in common with Mesoamerican solar deities. Just as the sun was eternally threatened by nocturnal forces, Christ was put to death by his persecutors. His ascent to Heaven each Easter could therefore be seen as the victory that guaranteed his followers another year of life on earth.

opposite
Holy Week procession in the highland town of Pahuatlán, Puebla state, 1986. The figures of Christ and the Virgin Mary are carried through the streets. Young men, dressed as Roman centurions and carrying lances, accompany the procession.

Ash Wednesday and Lenten ceremonies usher in the period known as *Semana Santa* (Holy Week). The Friday before Holy Week is dedicated to the *Virgen de Dolores* (Our Lady of Sorrows). In early church history this feast was called 'The Seven Sorrows of the Blessed Virgin Mary', and she was often depicted with seven daggers in her heart. In streets, homes and churches, altars are erected to honour her life of suffering and sacrifice. Arranged near her image are oranges, shiny glass spheres, gold foil, cut paper banners, candles and flowers. Grief is evoked by the colour purple, purity by the colour white, and Christ's blood by the colour red. Sprouting seeds and green shoots symbolize renewal and rebirth.

On *Domingo de Ramos* (Palm Sunday), the faithful attend a special mass which includes the blessing of palm fronds and palm crosses. This commemorates the Saviour's entry into Jerusalem and marks the start of Holy Week. Some of the blessed palms are later burned and the ashes reserved by the church. They will be used the following year on Ash Wednesday to mark the sign of the cross on the foreheads of communicants. The Last Supper is recalled on Maundy Thursday, followed by Christ's trial and crucifixion on *Viernes Santo* (Good Friday) – the saddest day of the year for Christians. *Sábado de Gloria* (Saturday of Glory) ends with Christ's Resurrection. Every church in Mexico is packed on *Domingo de Pascua* (Easter Sunday), as celebrants share a sense of spiritual renewal. Until the moment of the Resurrection, however, church bells everywhere remain silent. Artisans and toymakers have traditionally made *matracas* (rattles) for the days of mourning. Fashioned from wood, tin, horn and bone, they have a cogged wheel. When the *matraca* is spun, the wheel strikes a projecting strip to produce a deafening noise. Some *matracas* are shaped like parrots or fish; others may be decorated with images from *la lotería*.

opposite
Painted pottery sculpture of the Last Supper from Ocumicho, Michoacán state, mid 1980s. The apostles are eating watermelon and other Mexican foods. Ceramic work from this celebrated Purépecha village is mostly made by women and is highly imaginative. Ht 32.5 cm.

below
Painted pottery figure of Christ from the Purépecha village of Ocumicho, Michoacán state, mid 1980s. Ht 46 cm.

Judas figures, so-called in memory of Judas Iscariot, are sold and sometimes ritually burned to celebrate the Resurrection. Frederick Starr, the North American ethnographer, described the custom in the late 1890s:

> It is on the day before Easter, the Saturday of Glory, that gaiety reaches its culmination in the public destruction of Judas, the betrayer. For three days or so beforehand, street vendors have sold these figures by thousands. They are of all sizes, forms and grades. Some are dressed in charra suits, some are in soldier-uniforms, some are horned and tailed to represent the devil: some are beggars and some are fine gentlemen: some are fat and some are lean. They range from a few inches to ten feet, or more, in length. They are composed of card or paper-pulp, and have fireworks (*cuetes*, or rocket-crackers) worked into or on them. They are hung over the middle of the street and exploded at noonday. They are often filled with things for the rabble — meat, soap, bread, clothing, candy, etc. The people scramble for these, and run their chances of being hurt by the exploding *cuetes* ...

Much has changed in Mexico since the 1890s, but small Judas figures of papier mâché are still made in Mexico City and the state of Guanajuato. Makers, known as *Juderos*, often base their designs on old models. As in Starr's time, small Judas figures usually represent red-painted devils or moustachioed male figures dressed as *charros* (horsemen) and soldiers. Some human figures have animal heads, and this gives them a surreal appearance. A government ban on the sale of gunpowder in urban areas has limited the public burning of large Judas figures, but members of the extensive Linares family have special permission to mount this event on the street where they live, behind the *mercado de Sonora* in Mexico City. Felipe Linares Mendoza takes great pride in the tradition:

> When I was four or five years old, I would watch my father – Pedro Linares Jiménez – make Judas figures. By the time I was eight, I was helping him. It was

opposite

Gigantic Judas figures behind the Sonora Market in Mexico City on the Saturday of Glory, 1992. Makers construct a cane armature, then cover it with layers of paper stuck down with *engrudo* (flour-and-water paste). Here, fireworks are being attached to a *charro* (horseman).

the custom, in those days, to set light to Judas figures at ten in the morning on the Saturday of Glory. In the *pulquerías* it was a great fiesta: they would hang out Judas figures with measures of *pulque*. Shoe shops would attach gifts of shoes. Butchers would deck them out with cuts of meat. Now shops and businesses no longer do this. But the burning of Judas figures is still a fine sight. To construct the really big figures we use cane, twine, pitch, papier mâché, flour-and-water paste to glue the paper, and paints. When you make a Judas figure, you know it will be burned. People enjoy watching fire destroy the figures that I make.

Because of a change in church procedure, the Resurrection is now celebrated in the evening. As dusk falls on the Saturday of Glory, Felipe Linares Mendoza and his neighbours bring out their huge figures. Up to

above left
Pascual Andrade Ramírez of Guanajuato City in 2006. Moulds are used for these small-scale Judas figures of papier mâché.

above right
Gigantic Judas figures commissioned from Felipe Linares Mendoza in 1992. To the right of the devil is Blue Demon, a famous wrestler. Both figures are being collected from Felipe's home in Mexico City.

opposite
Brightly painted Judas figure of papier mâché. This green-eyed devil, with a long tail and decorated wings, was made *c.* 1989 in Mexico City or Guanajuato state. Ht 123 cm.

3 m (10 ft) high, these can take a variety of forms. Skeletons and devils are often represented, as are disgraced public figures. These have included ex-president Carlos Salinas de Gortari, 'El Negro' Durazo (the former police chief of Mexico City) and Saddam Hussein. Sometimes, Judas-makers portray much-loved public figures such as Cantinflas, the comic character featured in Mexican films of the 1940s and 1950s, and popular wrestlers like El Santo or Blue Demon. Hung with fireworks, figures are suspended from a rope above the road. When the touch-paper is lit, they disintegrate in a shower of sparks. Judas figures are donated by the makers, who are enriching the life of their community while also expressing their own religious faith. As Felipe's son Leonardo explains, the work of days is consumed in just a few minutes: 'Here in Mexico we value the ephemeral. Although we only have it for an instant, it remains embedded in the memory of the spectator.'

In many places, enormous effort goes into dramatizing the Passion. On Good Friday, in large towns and small villages, local people re-enact Christ's final ordeal. Iztapalapa, once a separate communuty but now part of Mexico City, attracts thousands of onlookers. The actor who plays Christ is selected for his good character and physical strength. Wearing a crown of thorns and dragging an immensely heavy cross, he is pursued through the streets and whipped by Roman soldiers. Eventually he is tied to a cross, high on the *Cerro de la Estrella* (Hill of the Star). On this spot, in pre-Christian times, the Aztecs performed the New Fire Ceremony to mark the end and beginning of each 52-year cycle.

Christ's sufferings are similarly represented, albeit on a less costly scale, in towns such as San Salvador Huixcolotla, Puebla. Maurilio Rojas, skilled in the art of cutting paper banners, remembers taking the role of Christ in the late 1980s as a young man. 'I felt deeply honoured to carry the cross and

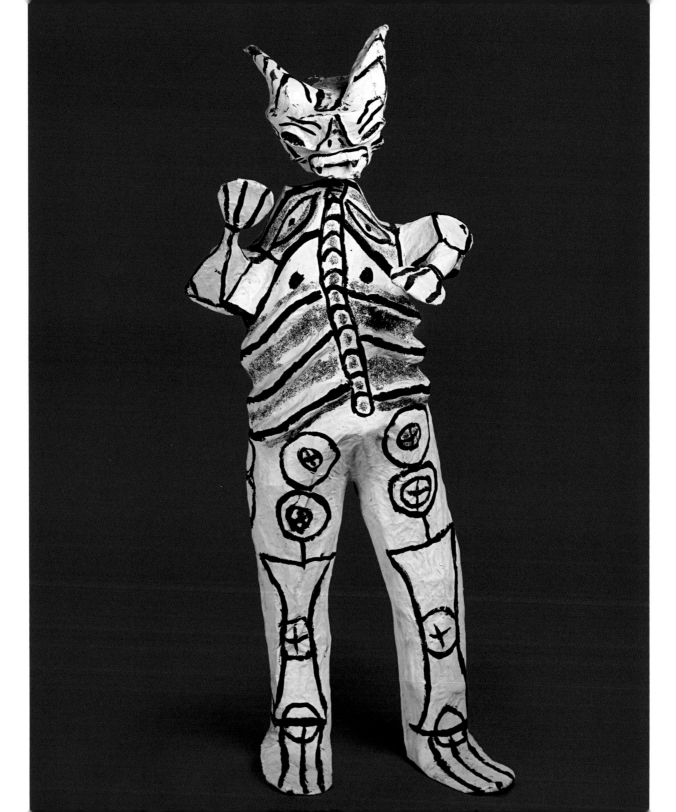

to follow in the footsteps of Our Saviour. I told my persecutors to hit me hard, so that I could feel something of what Jesus felt.' Frances Calderón de la Barca spent time in Mexico in the early 1840s, and she described the flagellation and bloody self-scourging of the *penitentes*. Although the Roman Catholic Church now discourages displays of public penance and self-imposed bodily suffering, pilgrims at the shrine of Atotonilco still pray and self-flagellate to atone for Christ's martyrdom. In Taxco, Guerrero, a similar endurance test is undergone by hooded young men who process carrying massive bundles of barbed *zarza* branches on their bare shoulders and outstretched arms.

Holy Week marks the beginning of the agricultural season for many farmers. Christ's miraculous resurrection parallels the regeneration of maize – the mainstay of life. Among the Mayo, the Yaqui, the Cora and the Tarahumara, *Semana Santa* ceremonies are syncretic, incorporating many pre-Christian beliefs and forms of expression. The Tarahumara, who refer to themselves as the Rarámuri, live in the state of Chihuahua among the precipitous peaks of the Sierra Madre Occidental. Religious teachings, introduced by Jesuit missionaries after 1608, have been reworked. According to the world view of the Tarahumara, their shamans and healers must maintain the sacred balance between different forces in the universe. *Semana Santa* is a very important festival. The Crucifixion story is re-enacted – with music, singing, dancing and processions – as a battle waged between malevolent *fariseos* (Pharisees) and good 'soldiers'. The *fariseos* paint their bodies white and wear white loincloths, red headbands and turkey feathers. Each group is led by captains. Eventually the forces of evil are vanquished.

The Cora, or Nayalita, were also assigned to the Jesuits. At Jesús María and other settlements in the state of Nayarit, *Semana Santa* is similarly envisaged as a battle. For young men, participation is a rite of passage from

opposite
Skeleton Judas figure of papier mâché, made in the mid 1980s by the late José Miranda Tinoco Caballero. His mother, Carmen Caballero Sevilla, created Judas figures for the artists Diego Rivera and Frida Kahlo. Ht 116 cm.

adolescence to adulthood. Christ's persecutors are represented by the *judíos* (Jews). Each performer is honour-bound to paint his body and construct a mask of papier mâché. The colour used for bodies and masks changes daily. On the Saturday of Glory, the *judíos* achieve purification by washing in the river and allowing the current to carry away their masks. As Ruth D. Lechuga has pointed out in *Mask Arts of Mexico*, the term *judío* does not refer to real people: 'In reality, the true significance of Holy Week for many unacculturated peoples is the cosmic struggle for life on earth. The *judíos* symbolize the nocturnal forces that kill the sun, as represented by Christ.' His ascent to Heaven is marked by general rejoicing. When performers pay homage to the new sun, they are hoping for a good harvest and a plentiful supply of food.

Holy Week ceremonies among the Mayo, or Yoremem, are equally rich in symbolism and have similar associations with agriculture. Settled along the Fuerte and Mayo rivers of northern Sinaloa and southern Sonora, the Mayo came under the influence of the Jesuit mission system in the 1590s. The elaborate public ceremonies that take place each year during Lent and Holy Week are a reaffirmation of Mayo identity. The organization of events depends upon a complex network of fraternities. These fraternities, with their different ranks and strict codes of conduct, appear to have combined the Jesuit talent for organization with the more ancient Mayo systems of military and civil government. Members are recruited by means of a ritual contract or *manda* with a saint. Christ is pursued, captured and symbolically crucified by youthful groups of *fariseos* (Pharisees) and *pilatos* (Pontius Pilates). The *pilatos* dress in black and cover their faces with masks of white cardboard; they also carry pointed lances and ride horses during festivities. The *fariseos* are foot-soldiers; their heads and shoulders are covered by helmet-like masks of hairy goatskin, shaved in parts and whitened so that features can be painted on to simulate animal or human faces.

'Pharisees' in the Mayo village of Bacabachi, Sonora state, 1978. During Holy
Week the *Pariserom* wear helmet-like masks of goatskin and jingling belts
hung with metallic cartridges. As Christ's captors and tormentors, they mock
everything the Mayo hold sacred. Yet the *Pariserom* are bound by a strict
code of conduct, and before ceremonies begin each Pharisee must take a vow of
silence. With Christ's Resurrection, they regain their humanity.

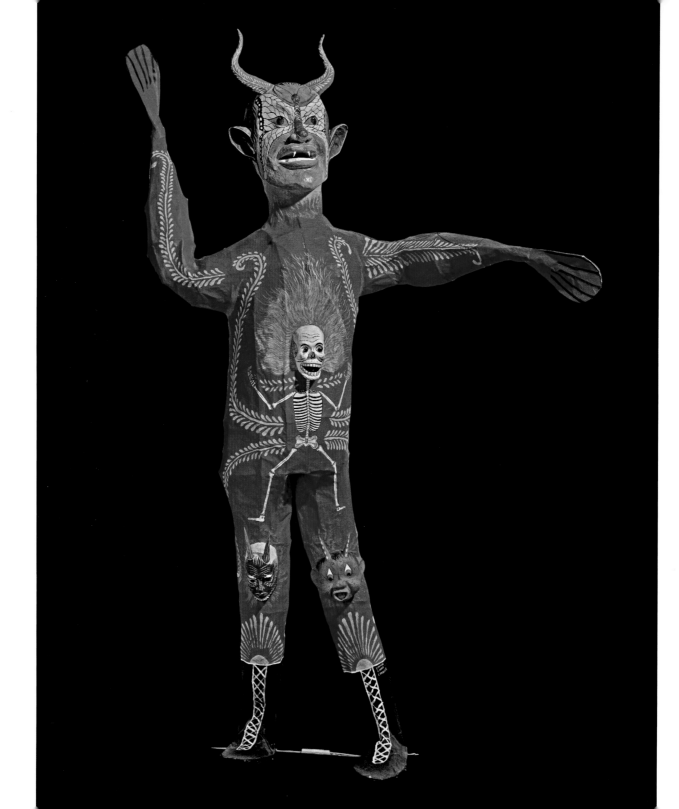

left
Banner of cut tissue paper showing the 'Lamb of God' (Agnus Dei). This visual representation of Jesus as a lamb with the holy cross reminds the faithful that their saviour shed his blood to atone for the sins of the world. Made *c.* 1989 by Maurilio Rojas of San Salvador Huixcolotla, Puebla state. 50 x 74 cm.

opposite
Gigantic Judas figure made by Leonardo Linares Vargas in 1992 during a residency at the Museum of Mankind in London. Layers of paper, stuck down with *engrudo* (flour-and-water paste), cover a cane armature. Ht 341 cm.

Throughout the period of Christ's suffering, *fariseos* and *pilatos* maintain their rule of evil. Only after the Resurrection does divine order reassert itself. As the bells ring out on the Saturday of Glory, the masked *fariseos* gather outside the church. Their rule ended, they sink to the ground. Each *fariseo* has spiritual 'godparents' who fan him with air. Holy water is sprinkled by a Mayo 'sacristan'. Freed at last from the malevolent forces that have possessed them, the *fariseos* hurl their masks on great bonfires where they are consumed by flames. Purification by air, fire and water is now complete. On Easter Sunday, the Mayo hold one last procession. Jesus and Mary, each represented by their image from the church, are brought together in a joyous *encuentro* (meeting). In the words of one participant, interviewed in Bacabachi in 1977, 'Each year we re-enact what happened long ago. Ever since I was born, I have been present at this feast. I took part as a child and now, aged seventy, I am still taking part. Christ gave his life for us, to save humanity. If he had not, there would be no humanity. This is our religion.'

The Days of the Dead:
Los Días de los Muertos

Viene la muerte cantando
Por entre la nopalera
En que quedamos, pelona,
Me llevas o no me llevas?

Death comes singing
Between the *nopales* (prickly pears)
What have we decided, bald one,
Will you or won't you take me?

Popular verse

Death is a frequent theme in Mexican popular culture. Although verses like this one convey a sense of familiarity and ironic detachment, Mexicans are as tormented by the idea of mortality as anyone else. The complex relationship that Mexico has with death was famously discussed by the poet Octavio Paz in *El laberinto de la soledad*, first published in 1959. Paz wrote: 'The word death is not pronounced in New York, Paris or London, because it burns the lips. The Mexican, by contrast, is familiar with death, jokes about it, caresses it, sleeps with it, celebrates it; it is one of his favourite toys and his most steadfast love. True, there is perhaps as much fear in his attitude as in that of others, but at least death is not hidden away …'

According to popular belief, the souls of the dead have divine permission to return each year to earth. On All Saints' Day and All Souls' Day (1 and 2 November) they take their place beside the living. This is not a sombre occasion, but a time for feasting and reunion. Although these days are determined by the Roman Catholic calendar, pre-Christian beliefs and practices are still an important force.

Death, for the ancient peoples of Mexico, signified not an end but a stage in a constant cycle. This cycle paralleled the yearly sequence of the seasons: after the dry period, when vegetation died, the rains brought new growth. The Aztecs, who rose to power after 1325, regarded life and death as complementary. Their world view was based on dualism, a system of balanced opposites. Life was aligned with strength, light and day; death was linked with weakness, darkness and night. Acutely aware of the changing

opposite
Sugar skull made for the Days of the Dead in Toluca, Mexico state, by Wenceslao Rívas Contreras, late 1980s. Ht 16.5 cm.

below
Painted pottery figure of a skeleton bull ridden by a devil and a human skeleton. Made *c.* 1989 by Abel Soteno Fernández of Metepec, Mexico state. Ht 44.5 cm.

seasons and nature's annual renewal, the Aztecs believed that existence was shaped by cycles of creation and destruction. Human blood was offered to the gods to maintain their life force. Without this vital nourishment, it was thought, the sun would lose the strength to rise each day. By these means, Aztec priests and rulers renewed the cycles of time and ensured the rebirth of life.

The afterlife was determined by the manner of death. Warriors who died on the battlefield were rewarded for their valour. They followed the celestial path of Tonatiuh, the sun god, from dawn until midday. After four years, they became hummingbirds. Women who died in childbirth, regarded as another form of battle, accompanied the sun from midday to dusk. Tlalocan, the lush and ever-green 'paradise' of the rain gods, was reserved for people who died a watery death. Dead infants went to a special place where a tree dripped milk from its leaves. These were exceptions, however. Most people were destined to make a hazardous, four-year journey to reach Mictlan – the cold and shadowy realm of the death god

left
Families decorating graves with flowers in the Zapotec village of San Antonino Castillo Velasco, Oaxaca state, 2001.

left

Painted pottery candelabrum in the form of a 'tree of life', featuring a skeleton orchestra. Musicians and surrounding decorations are supported on short lengths of wire. Made in the late 1980s by Heriberto Castillo Orta of Izúcar de Matamoros, Puebla state. Ht 104 cm.

below

Painted pottery whistle in the form of a skeleton figure holding its insides. Made in the mid 1970s in the Purépecha village of Ocumicho, Michoacán state. Ht 16.5 cm.

Mictlantecuhtli and his female counterpart Mictecacihuatl. The Aztec year, divided into eighteen twenty-day periods, included several feasts associated with cults of the dead. Miccailhuitontli and Miccailhuitl, held in the ninth and tenth months, honoured the Little Dead and the Adult Dead with feasting and dancing. Flowers were strung together; offerings of food included *tamales* (steamed cakes of maize dough) made with the meat of dogs and turkeys.

The Aztecs were not alone in their religious beliefs. As the inheritors of cultural traditions that were many centuries old, they shared their cosmology and their pantheon of gods with the other inhabitants of ancient Mexico. Representations of skulls, skeletons and human sacrifice abound – not just in central Mexico, but on the Gulf Coast and among the Maya. After AD 150, the preoccupation with death intensified. Ballcourts, where life-and-death ballgames were played, often displayed carved stone panels. At El Tajín

opposite

A yearly market for the Days of the Dead is held early on 31 October in Huaquechula, Puebla state, 1989. Villagers buy ceremonial pottery, candles, incense, sugar figures and flowers to receive the returning souls. *Tagetes erecta*, the Mexican marigold (*cempoalxochitl* in Nahuatl), is often referred to in Mexico as 'the flower of the dead'.

below

Sugar skulls for the Days of the Dead, made in the late 1980s in Toluca, Mexico state. Eye sockets are embellished with metallic foil. The maker, Wenceslao Rívas Contreras, is a celebrated sugar-worker who constantly invents new designs. Sugar figures are sold in Toluca each year during *la feria del alfeñique* (Sugar-paste Fair). Ht (left) 16.5 cm, (right) 8 cm.

in Veracruz and Chichén Itzá in Yucatán, scenes of human sacrifice evoked new life. Serpents, and a flowering plant bearing fruit, were shown issuing from the neck of a sacrificial victim at Chichén Itzá.

In Christian Europe, mortality was viewed very differently. Although death was seen as a journey, the destination was governed by moral precepts and by the Last Judgement. While the virtuous could aspire to heavenly bliss, eternal damnation awaited the sinner. All Saints' Day and All Souls' Day have been celebrated on 1 and 2 November since the fourteenth century or earlier. Inextricably linked, they honour Christian saints and commemorate the 'faithful departed' who die as good Christians. Over time, especially in southern Italy and Spain, both feasts accumulated beliefs and practices deemed 'unorthodox' by the Church. On 2 November, souls were popularly thought to come back from heaven to bless the households where they had lived. To welcome them and gain their protection, the living would set out offerings of food in cemeteries.

In New Spain, the feasts of All Saints' and All Souls' combined cultural traits from Europe – both orthodox and unorthodox – with pre-existing traditions. Writing in the late sixteenth century, the Dominican friar Diego Durán noted with regret that these Christian festivals had Aztec undertones. As he watched celebrants make offerings of chocolate, candles, fowl and fruit, Durán guessed that they were perpetuating pre-Hispanic rites for the dead. The cultural fusion has since been so complete that it would be difficult to determine today which aspects of the festival were introduced from Christian Europe and which aspects characterized the indigenous cult of the dead.

Although the festival varies from region to region, it is always regarded as a time of remembrance and renewal. For a brief period, the living join together with relatives and friends to welcome back the souls of the departed. Believers say they feel a sense of peace; they cannot see or speak

Black-glazed pottery *incensario* (incense burner) for the Days of the Dead, made by Alfonso Soteno Fernández of Metepec, Mexico state. Decorative elements, including the emblem of the Virgin of Guadalupe, are supported on short lengths of wire. Ht 41.5 cm.

left

Eugenio Reyes Eustaquio is a specialist maker of ceiling-high, all-white constructions for the 'new dead' in Huaquechula, Puebla state. In 1991 he built this splendid example at the Museum of Mankind in London for the exhibition 'The Skeleton at the Feast: The Day of the Dead in Mexico'.

below

Incensario (incense burner) of painted pottery, made in the late 1980s by Heriberto Castillo Orta of Izúcar de Matamoros, Puebla state. Decorative elements are suspended on wires. San Rafael, positioned on the rim, is one of the most important archangels in the celestial hierarchy. The protector of the young, the wayfarer and the pilgrim, he is often shown with a fish.

left
Painted pottery candle holder for the Days of the Dead, made in the late 1980s by Ignacio Peralta Soledad of Huaquechula, Puebla state. The Virgin Mary is surrounded by angels and *putti*. Ht 39.5 cm.

opposite
Painted sculpture of papier mâché and wire: an angel, a devil and a skeleton ride a bicycle. Made in 1989 by Saulo Moreno, who lives in Tlalpujahua, Michoacán state. Born in Mexico City in 1933, he is one of the most imaginative and innovative popular artists in Mexico. Ht 32.5 cm.

with the dead. Flowers, incense, candles, fruit, sugar figures, favourite foods and alcohol are set out on the domestic altar – usually a table for Catholic saints and holy pictures. Sometimes special objects are displayed: a feeding bottle for a dead baby, a newly embroidered blouse for a much-missed mother, or a father's machete. It is thought that the dead extract the 'essence' from these offerings, which are later used by the living. On the morning of 2 November, when the souls depart for another year, the bereaved visit the graveyard to say farewell with flowers and music.

The Days of the Dead are celebrated with considerable care throughout the central valleys of Oaxaca. Crispina Navarro Gómez, a distinguished weaver, lives in the village of Santo Tomás Jalieza (see p. 10). Her father died in 1985, and his return is eagerly awaited by the family each year. Cost, as Crispina explains, should never be an issue:

> My father worked in the fields, with no regular salary, but he never neglected this day. We follow his example. We set up our altar on 31 October to welcome the souls of dead children. On 1 November we put out offerings for all our departed. Most of all we do this for my father, but everyone is welcome. It is like a holiday. We put out flowers, incense, bread, chocolate – all the things they enjoyed in life. We also prepare *mole*. Next day we remove the food, but everything else stays in place for eight days. On 2 November we visit the cemetery. At noon, the bells sound. We experience a kind of tranquility. Those who are leaving us must surely feel tranquil too, knowing that we are well.

The ancient town of Huaquechula lies near the Popocatépetl volcano in the state of Puebla. Although most able-bodied men spend long periods of

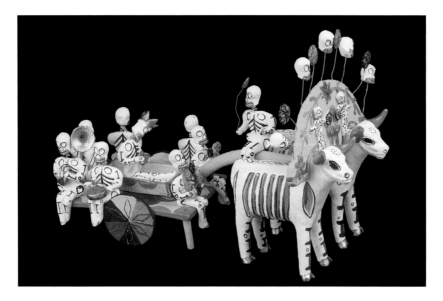

left
Painted pottery scene made by Abel Soteno Fernández of Metepec, Mexico state, mid 1980s. Skeleton oxen, fitted with a decorated yoke, pull a cart carrying skeleton musicians. In Metepec during the festival of San Isidro, carts are traditionally adorned with seed-pictures and flowers.
Ht (approx.) 21 cm.

opposite
Sculpture of papier mâché and wire made in 1989 by Saulo Moreno of Tlalpujahua, Michoacán. A devil and a skeleton converse with a 'lady of the night' beneath a lamppost. Ht 39.5 cm.

time away from home, seeking work in Mexico City or the USA, they try to return for the Days of the Dead. As in other places, family members set out offerings of food and flowers to welcome the returning souls. Unusually, however, the inhabitants of Huaquechula have also developed a monumental *ofrenda* (sometimes described by locals as an 'altar') for those who have died during the preceding year. Although some are free-standing, most are erected against a wall in the principal room. Over a structure of tables, wooden boxes and planks, approximately 80 m (260 ft) of white satin are draped, pleated and ruched. Pride of place is given to the photograph, if one exists, of the deceased. Ideally, this should be seen reflected in a mirror. Before the food offering is set out, ornaments of various kinds are added. These include a profusion of plaster angels and *llorones* (weeping children). It is not known how this style of offering evolved. The form may derive from the tiered funerary catafalques of the colonial period, while the white satin covering calls to mind the interior of modern coffins.

These spectacular, ceiling-high constructions for the 'new dead' are built by specialist makers, respected for their inventiveness and skill. Eugenio Reyes Eustaquio learnt the art of altar-making from his grandfather and his father. Interviewed in 2008, Eugenio offered the following explanation:

> Altars may vary in their design, but they all have three levels. One shows the earth, where we live. Next comes the separation: the physical from the spiritual. And lastly Heaven. These three levels define each altar. Because the offering is symbolically shared by the living and the dead, food is important. Here in Huaquechula, we give all our visitors something to eat and drink. The outlay is considerable. This year the cost of an average altar, including meals, will reach 35,000 or even 40,000 pesos. But a farm worker is paid just 125 or 130 pesos per day. Many families go into debt to meet their obligations. In order to receive our dead, great efforts and many sacrifices are made. This is our custom, as believers.

above
Skeleton fire-eater of papier mâché, from Mexico City, late 1980s. Ht 69 cm.

opposite
Exquisitely painted skull of papier mâché, featuring a lizard, a flowering branch and a *maguey* (agave). Made in 1989 in Mexico City by Felipe Linares Mendoza, who associates this type of skull with springtime, new growth and regeneration. Ht 38 cm.

The Days of the Dead are a focus for many arts and crafts, and makers throughout Mexico start production weeks or even months in advance. Work, generally unsigned, is often sold far from its place of origin. Yet it is the output of these 'anonymous' creators which gives the festival its unique character and visual power. As mid October approaches, markets fill with incense burners, vases and candle holders, embroidered cloths, cooking vessels and cut paper banners. Makeshift stalls in towns such as Toluca sell sugar skulls and figures in the shape of guitars, sheep, angels and souls in purgatory.

Dead children, known as *angelitos* (little angels), may be offered seasonal toys for the Days of the Dead. More usually, however, these toys are intended for the living. Toy-makers and miniaturists in several states fashion humorous playthings that move in ingenious ways. Photographs and written accounts from the late nineteenth century show that the custom is not new. Today, as in the past, markets in Oaxaca, Puebla and Mexico City

above left
Bone carving, mid 1980s, by Roberto Ruiz (1928–2008). Born in Miahuatlán, Oaxaca state, this celebrated miniaturist spent his adult life in Ciudad Nezahualcóyotl near Mexico City. *La Catrina* is flanked at the base by Death and the Devil. Ht 12 cm.

above right
La Catrina (c. 1890) is one of an estimated 20,000 engravings by José Guadalupe Posada.

opposite
Painted pottery candelabrum made c. 1985 by Abel Soteno Fernández of Metepec, Mexico state. Pitchfork-wielding devils are surrounded by the flames of hell. Ht 50 cm.

  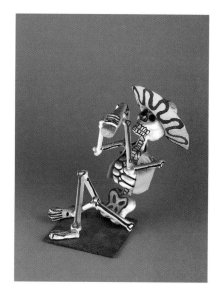

sell tiny coffins, cardboard skeletons that dance at the pull of a string, and clay skulls with movable lower jaws. Skeletons of painted clay caricature the activities of everyday life. They include musicians, wedding couples and bishops. In medieval Europe, paintings and carvings showed the 'dance of death'. In modern Mexico death is similarly regarded as an equalizer, striking down both rich and poor, powerful and weak.

The engravings of José Guadalupe Posada (1852–1913) are deeply rooted in the national culture. After an earlier career in Aguascalientes and León, Posada settled in Mexico City. From 1888, he supplied images to the capital's journal and book trades. His most important client was the printer-publisher Antonio Vanegas Arroyo. Working together for a mass market, they produced song sheets, devotional images and cheap scandal sheets. Today Posada is chiefly remembered for his mock obituaries known as *calaveras*. The *calavera* (literally 'skull') provided an opportunity for political satire and biting social comment. Sold during the Days of the Dead,

In urban Mexico the Days of the Dead inspire large numbers of popular artists. Those who work in papier mâché are often chroniclers of everyday life. Skeleton figures representing different social classes engage in a wide range of activities. They can also serve as a humorous vehicle for social comment.

above left
Skeleton office worker. Employed as a complaints clerk by the Mexican telephone service, he reacts with frustration when his own telephone fails to work. From Mexico City, late 1980s. Ht 34.5 cm.

above centre
Skeleton newspaper seller. From Mexico City, late 1980s. Ht 44 cm.

above right
Skeleton drinker. From Mexico City, late 1980s. Ht 25.5 cm.

these printed broadsides carried humorous verses. Accompanying images showed personalities and professions in the guise of skeletons. Although Posada was buried in a pauper's grave, his work was not forgotten. It found a new audience during the decades that followed the Mexican Revolution. *La Calavera Catrina* – perhaps his best known image – is now linked in the popular imagination with the festival of the dead. The Mexican artist Diego Rivera (1886–1957) paid tribute to Posada in his vast mural, *Dream of a*

Figures of painted pottery from Metepec, Mexico state. Death is the great equalizer: even the powerful and wealthy eventually become skeletons.

below left
Female skeleton by Mónico Soteno Fernández, *c.* 1988. Ht 64 cm.

centre and right
Life-size bishop and king by Tiburcio Soteno Fernández, 1989. Ht (centre) 170 cm, (right) 163.5cm.

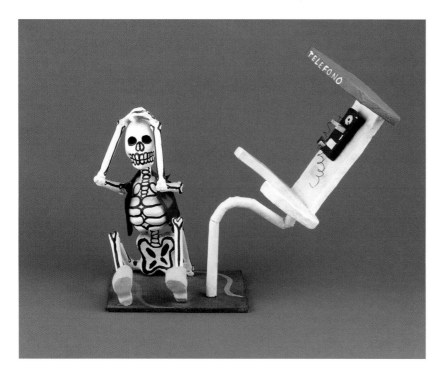

left
Skeleton figure of papier mâché finds the public telephone broken. From Mexico City, late 1980s. Ht 34 cm.

Sunday Afternoon in the Alameda Park (1947). *La Catrina*, shown full-figure, stands arm in arm with her creator Posada.

In more recent times, Posada's legacy can be seen in the papier mâché work of the Linares family and their many imitators. Felipe Linares Mendoza and his son Leonardo Linares Vargas – born in 1936 and 1963 respectively – live in the heart of Mexico City. Both are *cartoneros*, popular artists in papier mâché. So too are Felipe's other sons, David and Felipe junior. As a small boy, Felipe made seasonal toys and Christmas *piñatas* with his father, Pedro Linares Jiménez (1906–92). Later this range was extended to include interpretations of Posada's *calaveras*. Leonardo explains their enduring appeal: 'Although Posada lived a long time ago, his engravings seem up-to-date. Many people ask us to make three-dimensional skeletons based on

opposite right
Toy church of painted wood from Oaxaca state, mid 1980s. When a handle at the side is turned, the skeletons move their limbs. The bride and groom face each another across an altar resembling a funerary catafalque. The words read: *Día de Casamiento* (Wedding Day). Ht 43 cm.

opposite below
Painted wooden figures from the Zapotec village of Arrazola, Oaxaca state, mid 1980s. Three *soldaderas* (female soldiers from the 1910 Revolution) are shown as skeletons. Ht 20 cm.

Posada's images. He has been a source of inspiration for us. Sometimes we make modern-day, contemporary figures: punk-rockers, wrestlers, fire-eaters … But we also like to draw on the past.' Moulds are employed for the skulls and torsos of skeleton figures – later these are given their individual characteristics. Felipe and his sons are never depressed by their work: 'We don't find it sad. But then we don't regard the Day of the Dead as sad. We feel joyful when this day arrives each year, because we remember the departed and pay them homage.'

Saulo Moreno is also inspired by death. Born in 1933 and entirely self-taught, he fashions highly distinctive figures using wire, paper, flour-and-water

paste and car paints. Smaller figures are made from cast and soldered metal. Although Saulo often creates animals and birds, real and invented, death has always been his favourite theme:

> Life and Death are the eternal duality. In Mexico we never tire of representing death. When I was a child, I played with skulls and skeletons. Perhaps we are preparing ourselves psychologically for the final step. The physical fact of death is terrible, of course. As the saying goes: 'You are dust, and to dust you will return.' I am afraid of dying, just as other people are. But I share my daily life with death – I show her doing different things. For me, death is female. One must never laugh at death. She deserves our absolute respect. God, for most people, is male. But for me she is also a woman. She gives life, and she takes it away. We are born of woman, then we return to Mother Earth. When we die, our bodies decompose: they feed the earth and are reborn. We are all part of this constant cycle of death and regeneration.

above
Funeral scene of painted pottery from Metepec, Mexico state, late 1980s. Ht (priest) 16 cm.

opposite
Painted pottery 'tree of life' from Metepec, Mexico state, made by Tiburcio Soteno Fernández in 1989. It depicts the cycle of life and death. Family life and nature's bounty are shown on the lowest level; immediately above is a death-bed scene. The afterlife awaits: souls migrate towards heaven (presided over by God the Father), hell and purgatory. On All Souls' Day the dead arrive as skeletons to enjoy offerings of food and drink. Ht 109 cm.

Further Reading

ANCIENT MEXICO

Broda, Johanna, 'Festivals and Festival Cycles' in *Oxford Encyclopedia of Mesoamerican Cultures: The Civilizations of Mexico and Central America*, vol. 1, Oxford University Press, 2001

Coe, Michael D., *Mexico: From the Olmecs to the Aztecs*, Thames & Hudson, 2008

Durán, Fray Diego, *Book of the Gods and Rites and the Ancient Calendar*, ed. and trans. Fernando Horcacitas and Doris Heyden, University of Oklahoma Press, 1971

Kirchhoff, Paul, 'Mesoamérica sus Límites Geográficas' in *Acta Americana* I, 1943, pp. 92–107

Matos Moctezuma, Eduardo, Felipe Solis Olguín *et al*, *Aztecs*, Royal Academy of Arts, 2002

McEwan, Colin, *Ancient American Art in Detail*, British Museum Press, 2009

McEwan, Colin and Leonardo López Luján (eds), *Moctezuma: Aztec Ruler*, British Museum Press, 2009

Sahagún, Fray Bernardino de, *General History of the Things of New Spain* (Florentine Codex), ed. and trans. Charles E. Dibble and Arthur J.O. Anderson, 13 vols, Santa Fe School of American Research and University of Utah, 1950–82

COLONIAL AND 19TH-CENTURY MEXICO

Ajofrín, Francisco de, *Diario del viaje que hizo a la América en el siglo XVIII el P. Fray Francisco de Ajofrin*, Galas de Mexico, 1964

Calderon de la Barca, Frances, *Life in Mexico, during a Residence of Two Years in That Country (1843)*, Dent and Sons, 1970

Cervantes, Fernando, *The Idea of the Devil and the Problem of the Indian: The case of Mexico in the sixteenth century*, Institute of Latin American Studies, Research Paper 24, University of London, 1991

Díaz del Castillo, Bernal, *The True History of the Conquest of New Spain*, ed. Genaro García, trans. Alfred Percival Maudslay, 5 vols, Hakluyt Society, 1908–16

Gibson, Charles, *The Aztecs under Spanish Rule: A History of the Indians of the Valley of Mexico 1519–1810*, Stanford University Press, 1964

Lafaye, Jacques, *Quetzalcoatl and Guadalupe: The Formation of Mexican National Consciousness, 1531–1813*, trans. Benjamin Keen, University of Chicago Press, 1976

Ricard, Robert, *The Spiritual Conquest of Mexico: An Essay on the Apostolate and the Evangelizing Methods of the Mendicant Orders in New Spain, 1532–1572*, University of California Press, 1974

Taylor, William B., 'Cristos de Caña' in *Oxford Encyclopedia of Mesoamerican Cultures: The Civilizations of Mexico and Central America*, vol. 1, Oxford University Press, 2001

CONTEMPORARY MEXICO

Benson Gyles, Anna and Chloë Sayer, *Of Gods and Men: Mexico and the Mexican Indian*, BBC Publications, 1980

Crumrine, N. Ross, *The Mayo Indians of Sonora: A People who Refuse to Die*, University of Arizona Press, 1977

Crumrine, N. Ross and Marjorie Halpin, *The Power of Symbols: Masks and Masquerades in the Americas*, UBC Press, 1983

Horcacitas, Fernando, *The Aztecs Then and Now*, Editorial Minutiae Mexicana, 1979

Lipp Jr, Frank J., 'Zoque' in *Oxford Encyclopedia of Mesoamerican Cultures: The Civilizations of Mexico and Central America*, vol. 3, Oxford University Press, 2001

Madsen, William, *Christo-Paganism: A Study of Mexican Religious Syncretism*, Publication No. 19, Middle American Research Institute, Tulane University, 1957

Madsen, William, 'The Nahua' in *Handbook of Middle American Indians*, vol. 8, ed. Evon Z. Vogt, University of Texas Press, 1969

Madsen, William, *The Virgin's Children: Life in an Aztec Village Today*, University of Texas Press, 1960

Nutini, Hugo G., 'Syncretism' in *Oxford Encyclopedia of Mesoamerican Cultures: The Civilizations of Mexico and Central America*, vol. 3, Oxford University Press, 2001

Paz, Octavio, *The Labyrinth of Solitude: A Dramatic Portrait of the Mexican Mind*, trans. Lysander Kemp, Allen Lane, Penguin Press, London, 1967

POPULAR ART AND CULTURE

Artes de México, *The Crafts of Mexico*, Smithsonian Books in association with Artes de México, 2004

Espejel, Carlos, *Las artesanías tradicionales en México*, Secretaría de Educación Pública, 1972

Espejel, Carlos, *Cerámica popular mexicana*, Editorial Blume (photography by F. Catala Roca), 1975

Espejel, Carlos, *Juguetes mexicanos*, SEP/FONAPAS, Secretaría de Educación Pública, 1981

Espejel, Carlos, *Mexican Folk Crafts*, Editorial Blume, 1978

Fomento Cultural Banamex, AC, *Grandes Maestros del Arte Popular Mexicano*, 1994

Masuoka, Susan N., *En Calavera: The Papier-Mâché Art of the Linares Family*, UCLA Fowler Museum of Cultural History, 1994

Mulryan, Lenore Hoag *et al*, *Ceramic Trees of Life: Popular Art from Mexico*, UCLA Fowler Museum of Cultural History, 2003

Oettinger, Marion Jr, *Folk Treasures of Mexico: The Nelson Rockefeller Collection*, Harry N. Abrams, 1990

Orellana, Margarita de *et al*, 'Rituales del Maíz', *Artes de México*, no. 78, 2006

Orellana, Margarita de *et al*, 'El arte traditional del Nacimiento', *Artes de México*, no. 81, 2006

Sayer, Chloë, *Arts and Crafts of Mexico*, Thames and Hudson, 1990

Sayer, Chloë, *Crafts of Mexico*, Aldus Books, 1977

Sayer, Chloë, 'Saulo Moreno: An Interview with Chloë Sayer' in 'New Art from Latin America: Expanding the Continent', *Art & Design Magazine*, Academy Group, 1994

Sayer, Chloë *et al*, 'Metepec y su Arte en Barro', *Artes de México*, no. 30, 1995–6

Starr, Frederick, Catalogue of a Collection of Objects Illustrating the Folklore of Mexico, Published for the Folk-Lore Society by David Nutt, 1899

Toor, Frances, *A Treasury of Mexican Folkways*, Crown Publishers, 1976

HUICHOL CULTURE

Artes de México, 'Arte antiguo cora y huichol: La Colección de Konrad T. Preuss', *Artes de México*, no. 85, 2007

Furst, Peter T., 'Huichol' in *Oxford Encyclopedia of Mesoamerican Cultures: The Civilizations of Mexico and Central America*, vol. 2, Oxford University Press, 2001

Furst, Peter T. and Barbara G. Myerhoff, 'El mito como historia: el ciclo del peyote y la datura entre los huicholes' in *El peyote y los huicholes*, Sep-Setentas, no. 29, 1972

Lumholtz, Carl, *Unknown Mexico*, 2 vols, Macmillan, 1903

Myerhoff, Barbara G., *Peyote Hunt: The Sacred Journey of the Huichol Indians*, Cornell University Press, 1974

Negrín Fetter, Juan *et al*, 'Arte Huichol', ed. Johannes Neurath, *Artes de México*, no. 75, 2005

CHRISTIANITY AND OUR LADY OF GUADALUPE

Colle, Marie-Pierre, *Guadalupe: Body and Soul*, Vendome Press, 2005

Crumrine, N. Ross and Alan Morinis (eds), *Pilgrimage in Latin America*, Greenwood Press, 1991

Salvo, Dana *et al*, *Home Altars of Mexico*, William H. Beezley, 1997

Stafford Poole, C.M., 'Guadalupe, Nuestra Señora de: An Overview' in *Oxford Encyclopedia of Mesoamerican Cultures: The Civilizations of Mexico and Central America*, vol. 1, Oxford University Press, 2001

FESTIVALS, DANCES AND MASKING

Brandes, Stanley H., *Power and Persuasion: Fiestas and Social Control in Rural Mexico*, University of Pennsylvania Press, 1988

Cordry, Donald B., *Mexican Masks*, University of Texas Press, 1980

Crumrine, N. Ross, *El ceremonial de Pascua y la Identidad de los Mayos de Sonora*, Instituto Nacional Indigenista, 1974

Esser, Janet Brody, *Faces of Fiesta: Mexican Masks in Context*, San Diego University Press, 1981

Esser, Janet Brody, *Máscaras ceremoniales de los tarascos de la sierra de Michoacán*, Instituto Nacional Indigenista, 1984

Esser, Janet Brody (ed.), *Behind the Mask in Mexico*, Museum of International Folk Art and Museum of New Mexico Press, 1988

Gagnier de Mendoza, Mary Jane, *Oaxaca: Family, Food and Fiestas in Teotitlán* (photography by Ariel Mendoza), Museum of New Mexico Press, 2005

Henao Giraldo, Fernando and Everardo Gordillo Estrada, *Ceremonias Navideñas en la Cultura Popular*, Editorial de Antonio Vanegas Arroyo (no date)

Horcacitas, Fernando *et al*, *Lo Efímero y Eterno del Arte Popular Mexicano*, vol. 2, Fondo Editorial de la Plástica Mexicana, 1971

Hyman, Timothy, 'A Carnival Sense of the World' in *Carnivalesque*, Hayward Gallery Publishing, 2000

Lechuga, Ruth D., 'Carnival in Tlaxcala' in *Behind the Mask in Mexico*, Museum of International Folk Art and Museum of New Mexico Press, 1988

Lechuga, Ruth D., *Máscaras tradicionales de México*, Banco Nacional de Obras y Servicios Publicos S.N.C., 1991

Lechuga, Ruth D. and Chloë Sayer, *Mask Arts of Mexico*, Thames and Hudson, 1994

Mauldin, Barbara, 'Ritual and Play' in *¡Carnival!*, Museum of International Folk Art, 2004

Mauldin, Barbara, *Tigers, Devils, and the Dance of Life* (field photography by Ruth D. Lechuga), Museum of New Mexico Press, 1999

Mompradé, Electra L. and Tonatiúh Gutiérrez, 'Danzas y Bailes Populares', *Historia General del Arte Mexicano*, vol. 6, Editorial Hermes S.A., 1976

Romero Salinas, Joel, *La Pastorela Mexicana: origen y evolución*, SEP Cultura: FONART, 1984

Warman Gryj, Arturo, *La danza de moros y cristianos*, Sep/Setentas, 1972

Winningham, Geoff *et al*, *In the Eye of the Sun: Mexican Fiestas*, Norton, 1997

THE DAYS OF THE DEAD

Brandes, Stanley H., *Skulls to the Living, Bread to the Dead: The Day of the Dead in Mexico and Beyond*, Blackwell, 2006

Carmichael, Elizabeth and Chloë Sayer, *The Skeleton at the Feast: The Day of the Dead in Mexico*, British Museum Press, 1991

Garciagodoy, Juanita, *Digging the Days of the Dead: A Reading of Mexico's Días de Muertos*, University Press of Colorado, 1998

Lomnitz, Claudio, *Death and the Idea of Mexico*, Zone Books, 2005

Nutini, Hugo G., 'Day of the Dead and Todos Santos' in *Oxford Encyclopedia of Mesoamerican Cultures: The Civilizations of Mexico and Central America*, vol. 3, Oxford University Press, 2001

Nutini, Hugo G., *Todos Santos in Rural Tlaxcala: A Syncretic, Expressive, and Symbolic Analysis of the Cult of the Dead*, Princeton University Press, 1988

Pomar, María Teresa, *El Día de los Muertos: The Life of the Dead in Mexican Folk Art*, Fort Worth, 1987

Posada, José Guadalupe, *José Guadalupe Posada: Ilustrador de la vida mexicana*, Fondo Editorial de la Plástica Mexicana, 1963

Posada, José Guadalupe, *José Guadalupe Posada: Messenger of Mortality*, Redstone Press, 1989

Sayer, Chloë (ed.), *Mexico: The Day of the Dead*, Redstone Press, 1990

Illustrations

Index